UNIVERSITY OF NORTH CAROLINA AT CHAPEL HILL
DEPARTMENT OF ROMANCE LANGUAGES

NORTH CAROLINA STUDIES
IN THE ROMANCE LANGUAGES AND LITERATURES

Founder: URBAN TIGNER HOLMES
Editor: MARÍA A. SALGADO

Distributed by:

UNIVERSITY OF NORTH CAROLINA PRESS
CHAPEL HILL
North Carolina 27515-2288
U.S.A.

NORTH CAROLINA STUDIES IN THE
ROMANCE LANGUAGES AND LITERATURES
Number 236

CYCLOPEAN SONG

CYCLOPEAN SONG:
MELANCHOLY AND AESTHETICISM IN GÓNGORA'S *FÁBULA DE POLIFEMO Y GALATEA*

BY
KATHLEEN HUNT DOLAN

CHAPEL HILL
NORTH CAROLINA STUDIES IN THE ROMANCE
LANGUAGES AND LITERATURES
U.N.C. DEPARTMENT OF ROMANCE LANGUAGES
1990

Library of Congress Cataloging-in-Publication Data

Dolan, Kathleen Hunt.
  Cyclopean song: melancholy and aestheticism in Góngora's Fábula de Polifemo y Galatea / by Kathleen Hunt Dolan.
  p.   cm. – (North Carolina studies in the Romance languages and literatures; no. 236).
  Includes bibliographical references and index.
  ISBN 8078-9240-8
  1. Polyphemus (Greek mythology) in literature.   2. Galatea (Greek deity) in literature.   3. Melancholy in literature.   4. Aestheticism (Literature).
I. Title.   II. Series.
PQ6394.P63D65 1990
861'.3 – dc20   90-39387
                                                                                                            CIP

© 1990. Department of Romance Languages. The University of North Carolina at Chapel Hill.

ISBN 0-8078-9240-8

Depósito legal: v. 1.070 - 1990   I.S.B.N. 84-599-3025-4
Artes Gráficas Soler, S. A. - La Olivereta, 28 - 46018 Valencia - 1990

quae quoniam rerum naturam sola gubernas
nec sine te quicquam dias in luminis oras
exoritur neque fit laetum neque amabile quicquam,
te sociam studeo scribendis versibus esse . . .

CONTENTS

	Page
PREFACE	11
INTRODUCTION	17
I "GONGORISMO" AND THE CYCLOPS	21
1. *Gongorismo:* The Peacock and the "light in things"	21
2. The Cyclops and His Classical Lineage	42
II THE CAVERN AND THE SOLAR EYE	53
1. The "caverna profunda"	53
2. The "melancólico vacío": Time, Subjectivity and Melancholy	60
3. The Underworld and Formal Deficiency	68
4. The Cavern and the Solar Eye	70
III SATURN AND VENUS	79
1. Saturnine Melancholy and the Venusian Realm	79
2. Cyclopean Song	87
3. Venus and the "Reino de la espuma"	96
IV CONCLUSION	107
1. Polarities: a Recapitulation	107
2. Cyclopean Language	110
3. Poetry and Mediation	113
4. The Heraldry of the Imagination	120
WORKS CITED	132

PREFACE

How could we fail to be drawn to a poet whose work was denounced by contemporaries as "delirious," "pestilential," and "fraudulent"? In response to the attacks that followed upon the circulation of his two long poems, the *Fábula de Polifemo y Galatea* and the *Soledades* (whose relation to one another suggests somewhat the relation of *Ulysses* to *Finnegan's Wake*), Góngora made what has always seemed to me a rather unconvincing defense of his poetics in his often-quoted "Carta en Respuesta" (1613 or 1614). His poems are justified, he feels compelled to say, by their usefulness as mental exercise – they serve to *avivar el ingenio*, enliven the wit. Moreover, the serious and attentive reader will look below the surface of his verse and uncover their mystery, "lo misterioso que encubren." After all, Ovid, the Hellenistic Góngora, was also difficult and "obscure," but repaid the efforts of the diligent with a deepened power of understanding.

The "mystery which they conceal" would seem to have been designed to entice and entangle critics whose theoretical equipment has so far ranged from Neoplatonism to "Marxist-structuralism," hinting as it does at allegorical levels of meaning which no one, in over three centuries of published commentary, has been able to convincingly conjure forth from his reverberant, densely allusive verse. And surely Góngora's remarks in this very official letter are not only unpersuasive but misleading. For, after all, the poet is constrained to defend himself within the terms set by his detractors and by the prevailing literary ideology which they upheld, which collided so noisily with his extravagant and visionary language.

The fact is that the expressive power of Góngora's verse far outstrips his capacity for defending, in prose, its unsettling exhibition: the winged pedantry of the former drags its feet in the latter. So perhaps we should attend to his earliest critics, and rejoice in what they deplored: that although the veil is occasionally ripped away to reveal the ghostly face of Truth, linguistic bedazzlement in the service of wonder at *what is there*, at the things that suffice, generally prevails over doctrinaire sobriety.

Concerning Góngora's relations to the culture of seventeenth century Spain, or even to the useful concept "baroque," I have said little, except for remarks, in Chapter I, on the *Conceptista-Culteranista* controversy. It is well known that Góngora was a citizen of "España encantada," an almost surreally rhetorical culture staggering under the spell of Hapsburg repression and grandiosity; deluded, burnt-out, bankrupt and as we like to say — baroque. I refer the reader who would like to study *Gongorismo* as a feature of the "monarchical-seignorial pyramid" to José Maravall's detailed view of seventeenth century Spain in *Culture of the Baroque: Analysis of a Historical Structure*.

Private motives for writing a book must always be complex and probably never entirely understood by the author; certain images from the *Polifemo* haunted me throughout graduate school days, and the discrepancy between the psychic potency of those images and my own inadequate grasp of Góngora's difficult verse grew disturbing and provoking. I undertook this study in order to bring some light and order to the "caverna oscura" of my attraction to the poem. If I have not succeeded in "demystifying" its charisma — I hope I have not — or in making the poem more accessible to even the favorably disposed reader, then it may be that my enthusiasm was destined to be a private one, and that the poem has once more succeeded as a paradigm of blissful evasion.

I began the first draft of this book in the rainy Irish summer of 1985, seated in the tiny Sligo library with the poem and a pile of notes (no books, though shelves nearby, teeming with works on certain Irish Modernists, may have provided unsolicited and perhaps subversive inspiration). At that time it was the polarity of the Venusian and the, as I have seen it, Saturnine which most intrigued me. The contrast of monstrosity and beauty which Dámaso Alonso so eloquently delineates in his study of the poem seemed to hint at a world of meaning which might be illumined by a closer look at classical sources. I tried to coordinate readings from these texts or passages with clues found in the work on melancholy by Panofsky, Saxl and Klibansky. Ficino too offered unexpected insights into the psychic patterns and cultural import of the "Saturnine type."

Heidegger crept in later (no one has yet presented us with an "existential" Góngora – I have not undertaken to do so) after Nietzsche, supreme thinker against Saturnine gravity, was well installed as a tutelary *geist*. For this, and for not re-tuning my material to the key of their more popular French successors, I beg the reader's indulgence.

Like the animals in Rilke's Eighth Elegy, the lovers in Góngora's Ovidian poem experience their lives as boundless, *unendlich*. They gaze out into vastness, into the "Open." But Polyphemus is human, and circumscribed. He gazes only at objects:

> .... Only *our* eyes are turned
> backward, and surround plant, animal, child
> like traps, as they emerge into their freedom.[1]

The stone-hurling Polyphemus is a nihilist and failed poet. He is also, like all nihilists, an "essentialist," since he burns for the totality of nothingness, an irrevocable negation, and end to all beginnings. His victim is reduced to fragments of bones and flesh, while the stone that kills him is compared to an "urn" and a "pyramid" – monumental reconstructions of the monster's rapacious eye. Polyphemus destroys a particular order – the order whose center is the bower of Acis and Galatea – and installs in its place not a superior structure but a gash, the bleeding limbs and slack mouth of the world, the world's body severed from its vanished soul. The illusory "nothing" he produces is quickly invaded by "something" – the pearly shimmer and flux of the Gongorine river (Ovid's is blue-green, and the figure of Acis, seen above the current, is still intact), composed of the liquified bones of Acis as they flow back into the circuit of the poem, the circuit of value. This reconstruction affirms existence as both contingency and value, flux and form. It also, as an assertion of renewed identity, comes close to what we mean by style; for style is the

---

[1] *Selected Poetry*. Trans. Stephen Mitchell. (N.Y.: Random House, 1984), p. 193.

formal deployment of the poet's characteristic psychic emphases and tensions in the face of the murderous gravity of the doctrinaire.

I have tried to be attentive to issues of style and form while remaining consistent in my involvement with what I view as the neglected meditative disposition of the poem; in so doing I have felt compelled to place the poem in relation to texts not usually associated with Góngora or even the Spanish Baroque. I can offer no justification for this method, if it is one, or for the omission of references to such important stylistic and thematic predecessors as Carrillo de Sotomayor and Fernando de Herrera. Some less quoted critics helped to point the way – Zdislas Milner and James Dauphiné, for example. And of course a significant debt is owed to Dámaso Alonso, who so deftly lay the foundations of modern Góngora criticism. And it is indeed the extraordinarily gifted and largely unaffiliated writers of his generation – Reyes, Lorca, Guillén, Salinas and others – who still seem to me to have best understood and explicated Góngora's poetics of contingency.

Articles by Colin S. Smith and Anthony Cascardi were also helpful; and, more indirectly, in the party of the non-Gongoristas, the work of Rosalie Colie. It would be hard to find more impressive – and intimidating – model for the type of study that considers pastoral poetry from philosophical, formal, and social perspectives than Colie's elegant and rigorous reading of Andrew Marvell, in which the tradition of pastoral is considered as a mode of thought and criticism. For the tradition of wit in Góngora the reader is directed to A. A. Parker's *conceptista* Góngora (listed in *Works Cited*), and to an earlier study by Elias Rivers, "El Conceptismo del 'Polifemo'."

While Góngora has long been suspected of a "monumental" poetics because he seems to use language like paint or marble or stained glass, the human voice in the *Polifemo* breaks through in the lyric impulse of the monster, disclosing the poem's dark interior: "Oh Galatea..." In this eruption into song is concentrated a whole world of human meaning, the unstable, insistent complex of meaning that informs yearning, the monstrous-human yearning towards an absolute that recedes like a mirage. Here it is the sea itself, focused in a single point of light – the desired nymph – which is the dimension of the unattainable Other. If I have not always been faithful to that voice, the voice which Góngora nearly submerges beneath the glittering textures of his poetic landscape, I take refuge in the suspicion that works of literary criticism are always doomed to fall away from their subjects, seizing and losing, as the Cyclops himself seizes and loses. Ecrivons, dupons-nous.

Seattle, 1989

INTRODUCTION

The art and poetry of the baroque age bestowed to cultural history an extraordinary array of powerful and resonant images, many of which transcend the particular vocabularies of their time to enter into a community of universal types. It is a premise of the present study that Góngora's baroque Cyclops, both more human and more monstrous than his Ovidian prototype of *Metamorphoses* XIII, has long deserved to take his proper place in this gallery of cultural symbols. The exceptional community of souls to which he claims membership encompasses a spectrum of extreme states of consciousness, ranging from abysmal fallenness and the agony of martyrdom to ecstasy and beatitude: Bernini's Saint Teresa, inky-cloaked Hamlet, the agonized martyrs of Zurbarán and Ribera, Caravaggio's Paul struck blind by the light of heaven, Don Juan in his defiance of God and man and death, Don Quixote "breaking out through the door of his madness."

Polifemo, the dark protagonist of Góngora's brilliant fable of eros, death and transformation, belongs among those who are found caught in the extremity of the human condition, swooning, soliloquizing, raging, betraying, dissembling, hallucinating, clamoring for impossible revelations.

But we are not concerned merely with an individual consciousness, a figure plucked from the web that constitutes its "ground," for the vehemence and theatricality of such types, their aura of spiritual crisis, more often than not extends beyond a characteristic posture – saintly ecstasy, sudden illumination, tragic dissent, manic denial of reality, etc. – to inform an encompassing space, a "field" of sorts within which they radiate their commanding presences. They open up a world, and are held within it. This is true despite the fact that each seems, in an age of histrionic individualism, on the verge of breaking from its given frame, a "figure" about to detach itself from its "ground." In this emphatic tension with their grounding they verge on the monstrous, the dissonant, and the unaccountable while they transform the space they inhabit.

Shakespeare's Caliban is, like Góngora's Cyclops, a creature who is associated with the lower powers of the earth. A savage, or "wild man" who has acquired the power of language through the intervention of the immigrant Prospero, he is contrived to represent a monstrosity restricted to the obviously deformed and marginally human. In many ways akin to the baroque Polyphemus, he is a primitive in internal exile from his own island. Though a captive both of Prospero and of his own creaturely limitations, he is occasionaly awarded a glimpse of paradise, as though in sleep the roof were to be lifted from his spiritual prison:

> Sometimes a thousand twanging instruments
> will hum about mine ears; and sometimes
> voices that if I then had waked after
> sleep, will make me sleep again; and then
> in dreaming, the clouds methought would open,
> and show riches ready to drop upon me, that
> when I waked I cried to dream again.
> (*The Tempest* III.2, 146-52)

Normally a creature of brute appetite, Caliban here testifies to a visionary experience of a transformed world. Like Polyphemus he is a "thing of darkness," mocked by paradise, by that luminous plane of existence which seems almost within his grasp, and which makes his own seem heavy and oppressive. He figures human existence as exclusion and monstrosity, privation relieved on occasion by transcendent vision.

Góngora's Cyclops too is a type of monstrous human singularity, cousin, within the specific cultural boundaries of baroque Spain, to Tirso de Molina's Don Juan of *El burlador de Sevilla*, and the equally volatile Segismundo of Calderón's *La vida es sueño*. He is, as we will see, more human than Caliban, but less so than these prodigies of the Spanish baroque stage. He is a primitive who appears on the threshold of the modern world, lumbering into an age of metaphysical obsessions carrying his varied antique baggage.

His appearance in the baroque age occurs within a specific, symbolic geography inherited from ancient pastoral and epic.

The outstanding features of the Cyclops' personal landscape not only define him in relation to the larger world he inhabits but figure the internal geography of the human psyche he represents. Its chief components are the cavern, which carries overtones of the periodic lapses toward original chaos in Hesiod's *Theogony*, and the watchtower-like cliff above the mirroring sea, upon which the Cyclops, beacon-like with his single bright eye, looms over both sea and Sicilian countryside. From this towering vantage point he enjoys an illusion of omnipotence and solidity and aspires to the conquest of his own melancholy. The giant goatherd is positioned both "below" and "above" the world, and his presence poses a colossal challenge to the exquisite formalism of Góngora's pastoral vision. The Cyclopean presence is the menace of subjective desire and purpose which open up a chasm in the earthly paradise of the Edenic couple. It makes a resonant content, an insistent, bellowing sound which must be silenced in order for the poem to resume its composure, and for the poet to complete his operation of levitation and metamorphosis.

CHAPTER I

"GONGORISMO" AND THE CYCLOPS

> "y oí desde tan métricas, armoniosas ventanas
> mis andaluzas fuentes de aguas italianas"
> Rafael Alberti, "A la pintura"

1. Gongorismo: The peacock and "the light in things"

We are not accustomed to think about the seventeenth century literary phenomenon known as *gongorismo* as a source of timeless images which draw our attention to fundamental issues of human existence; rather, it is more popularly assumed to be a freakishly mannered linguistic event whose relevance in our own age is limited to the group of Spanish poets known as the "generation of '27," for whom Luis de Góngora served as the high priest of the cult of the image. *Gongorismo*, or as it came to be known pejoratively in the seventeenth century, *culteranismo* (to echo *luteranismo* and so suggest a species of literary heresy [Collard 13] refers first of all to what was thought to be an abuse of latinisms and classical allusions. The comparison with religious heterodoxy was not new in the seventeenth century, as the rhetoric of an earlier reaction against Petrarchan innovations shows: Cristóbal de Castillejo's protest against the Italianate style of Garcilaso de la Vega invokes the menace of protestant schism, complaining that the "petrarquistas" of the early 1500's are a "new" and "strange" sectarianism comparable to that of the dread Luther. (Collard 74) The term "sect" is again taken up as a polemical weapon in the 1600's, as Quevedo, Cervantes, Tirso de Molina and others launch their attacks upon the degenerate Italianisms invading Spanish poetry. The critic Juan de Jáuregui refers to Góngora's verses as "rites" which are as alien to the native style in poetry as the Druidic is to Catholic ritual.[1] To the saturnine Quevedo Góngora's verses were "per-versos," true poetry perverted and lost "in an affected confusion of figurative language, and in an inundation of foreign words." (Collard 105-06)

The *culteranista* mode is typified by Góngora's two major poems, the *Fábula de Polifemo y Galatea* and the *Soledades*, whose dissemination in 1613 sparked a controversy which divided the Hispanic literary world into two camps whose savage and bitter polemics seem extraordinary to us today. The party which defended tradition and the "native style" of moral seriousness and plain, classical diction, argued that the Horatian *utile*, the didactic content of the work, should be firmly instated prior to the imaginative presentation of that work. The central thought of the poem, the subtle and compressed *concepto*, is compared by Jáuregui, leading critic of the "new style," to the "body" of the composition, which functions as the explication of the "matter," of *asunto*, the soul of the work. Ornament may then be applied, but kept strictly subordinate – as *dulce* is to *utile*. (Collard 32) Góngora sins against what Jáuregui designates "la religión poética" by scrambling the soul/body/ornament hierarchy. For Góngora, the soul of the work is its body, and the body is its allure, its appeal to the imagination. In the same troubling sense "concept," for Góngora, is inseparable from image, and is not plausible as an autonomous abstraction which may be adequately or extravagantly clothed. Hence "per-versos," verses which turn away from the doctrinal, from a foundation in a traditionally understood substance and truth.

At a time when the Spanish Empire was rapidly becoming a grandiose and decrepit way station for capital in the form of gold and silver on its way to Amsterdam and Genoa, literary patriots poised themselves to defend an ideal of robust and virile *castellanismo* (Lope de Vega, for example: "yo voy con la doctrina castellana" [Collard 13]). For these traditionalists the conflicting values of the "new" style and the "native" style line up according to a fantasy of national purity which is susceptible to infection by a deviant, effeminate and alien style:

---

[1] For a selection of relevant seventeenth century critical texts, see Ana Martínez Arancón's *La batalla en torno a Góngora*.

Culteranismo	*Castellanismo*
Obscurity	Clarity
Foreign	Native
New	Traditional
Body	Soul
Superfluous ornament	Essence or substance

According to those who upheld the tradition of an idealized, Castillian Spain and its severe *virtù*, the "new poetry" is an aberrant, intoxicated discourse in which the "body" of poetry turns away from its own soul and so becomes de-centered, un-grounded, a traitor to its privilege of metaphysical gravity.

Many of the rhetorical mannerisms of *gongorismo* – antithesis, complex metaphors, paramomasia – are nonetheless shared by the practitioners of the other dominant and sometimes rival literary mode of the period, *conceptismo. Conceptismo* denoted, from about 1460, simply the cultivation of the thought or idea, and became associated in the 1500's with a *style de point*, a subtle rhetorical style employing, among others, the figures just mentioned. Its central device is the ingenious metaphor, the best examples of which are to be found in Góngora himself, as we see in this décima, "De la *Fábula de Faetón* que escribió El Conde de Villamediana" (1617) which Dámaso Alonso calls "chemically pure *gongorismo.*" (2.123) The poet describes the river Po, where Phaethon was thought to have fallen to his death,

> Si trémulo no farol,
> túmulo de undosa plata.
> (Alonso, *'Polifemo'* 2.123)

[If not a tremulous lantern, then a tomb of undulating silver]

As the quavering light of a lighthouse, it draws the solar navigator – as though the sun were a moth drawn to the brilliant panes of the lighthouse – and as a tomb it encloses him. Villamediana's poem, the subject of Góngora's encomium, is imagined to contain the ashes of Phaethon, and is compared to a symmetrical golden urn perfect in its structural harmonies.

But the frequent emphasis on the vehicle of the metaphor inclines Góngora's conceits towards an *uprooting* of meaning: the result is that a unit of meaning which was thought to be enhanced by the device of the conceit yields place to the *déraciné* territory of the self-referring image. And so the essence of the conflict between the two literary movements seems to turn more on the fate of the "matter" which is left behind, rather than on the issues of the abuse of rhetorical figures, syntactical purity, or infection from foreign sources. Baltasar Gracián, otherwise an admirer of Góngora's mastery of the ingenious conceit, faults him for his failure to address moral issues. In the second book of his allegorical novel, *El Criticón*, "Crisi" IV, he publishes his criticism using the voice of the stoic sage Critilo

> Si en este culto plectro cordobés hubiera correspondido la moral enseñanza a la heroica composición, los asuntos graves a la cultura de su estilo, la materia a bizarría del verso, a la sutileza de sus conceptos, no digo yo de marfil, pero de un finísimo diamante merecía su concha. (2.29)

> [If, in this learned Cordovan plectrum, moral teaching had corresponded to heroic composition, gravity of substance to the culture of his style, matter to the elegant manner of his verse, to the subtlety of his conceits, then his conch would deserve to be formed not merely of ivory but of finest diamond.]

It has generally been acknowledged that *gongorismo* and *conceptismo* (the latter roughly equivalent to the English "metaphysical" style) cannot be strictly separated since they favor the same kind of conceptual subtleties the *agudezas* which are employed to hone the weapon of orthodoxy. However we must continue to be attentive to a fundamental distinction between the two, perceptively noted by Dámaso Alonso. Alonso's observations expose the root of a fundamental incompatibility that must be apprehended as not only stylistic but psychological, ideological, and even metaphysical, and which is best symbolized by the irreconcilable temperaments of Góngora and Quevedo. In an argument which carefully notes the inextricability of the two stylistic tendencies, Alonso observes that while both *conceptismo* and *culteranismo* express what he calls the baroque passion for the incongruous, and for complex and unstable or precarious structures, *culteranismo* manifests this habit of mind as a "llamarada hacia afuera," a yearning movement outwards, while *conceptismo* manifests the same underlying preoccupations by means of a language that tends to recoil from the physical world (Alonso 1.86). The former makes its appeal to the senses; the latter addresses itself to the "pure" intelligence of a disembodied mind, by means of the compressed and pointed thought or conceit, which may or may not bypass the concrete image.

Gracián, chief exponent of this style (and who exhaustively classifies the various types of *conceptos* in his *Agudeza y arte de ingenio*) positions a manifesto of his own *conceptista* program in his preface to *El criticón:* "Comienzo por la hermosa naturaleza, paso a la primorosa arte y paro en la útil moralidad." (I.8) His point of departure is "beautiful nature" (surface), exquisite artistry is the road and morality (depth, underlying meaning) is the goal. The movement of the strategy is from outer to inner, in the direction of intellect and spirit. Like the ingenuous Andrenio of Gracián's allegorical novel, who is dazzled by the spectacle of nature before his enthusiasm is curbed by the wise counsel of his mentor Critilo, the reader is deftly lured on by a rhetoric which recedes from itself, abdicating in favor of the invisible reality it serves. When the unenlightened Andrenio declares, in a burst of puerile enthusiasm, that his favorite color is green, the color most agreeable to sight (and long associated with Venus), Critilo disparages it as terrestrial and "humid," and re-directs his pupil's gaze to the incorruptible stars, beyond the "defective" and "stained" orbit of the moon. (I.26)

Gracián's heroes journey towards a liberation from contingency, and from journeying itself, which is redeemed by arrival on the "Island of Immortality" in the third book. *Gongorismo,* on the other hand, is an "oblique discourse" (a river in the *Soledad Primera* 1.200 is "torcido discurso) which branches and deviates; a discourse which resists, syntactically and rhetorically, arrival. And it affirms precisely those contingencies and corruptibilities which the senex Critilo rejects, and imposes upon the reader the role of perverse pilgrim wandering always within the orbit of the moon, and subject to its illusions, deviancies, and gratuitous display. Within this sublunary realm of illusion it is the quality of ostentation, of the peacock spreading its brilliant feathers, that has been responsible for much of the negative critical attention accorded *gongorismo* since 1613. For its aestheticism more than fulfills, especially in the florid silvas of the *Soledades,* Wallace Stevens's requirement for an "essential gaudiness" in poetry. The peacock once projected a dual symbolism in medieval Christian iconology: it was both a symbol of immortality – probably a western adaptation of the Oriental phoenix – and a symbol of worldly pride and vanity. (Ferguson 23) That Gracián is not so eager to abandon sublunary diversions as is his protagonist and mask Critilo, is evidenced by his fable "Hombre de ostentación," "Man of ostentation" (*El discreto* XIII) in which a peacock is made to defend himself against charges of ostentation by citing Genesis. His satisfaction in his splendid plumage is sanctioned by biblical cosmogony, for "tan presto era el luzir en las cosas como el ser." The impulse to self-display, Gracián tells us, is primordial and coeval with Being itself. The phrase "el luzir en las cosas," denotes an original light in things, independent of our perception of them. Surely the Jesuit moralist flirts with heterodoxy here, developing this bit of metaphysics – the coming into being of things and their shining forth as aspects of the same event – into the question "De qué sirviera la realidad sin la apariencia?" "What use is reality without appearance?"

Gracián's moral tale, and his ambivalence toward his subject, is ostensibly resolved with a compromise in the form of a judgement: Forced to adopt a humility which compromises the instinct to self-display common to all sentient beings, the peacock is condemned to contemplate his ugly feet each time he succumbs to the temptation to spread his brilliant feathers – "so that to raise up his plumage and to lower his eyes will be one and the same thing." The allegorization of the bird is complete: he will forever be conflicted, neurotic, *human*.

Even as he reforms the vanity of the peacock, Gracián praises the "art of seeming" which he liked to think was a peculiar and admirable trait of the Spanish people. For the artifice of self-presentation can be justified as a compensatory device, a necessary evil required for survival, though its sheer aesthetic allure clearly appeals to Gracián. So that although he is committed to a metaphysics which devalues appearances and to a Stoic ethics which cautions against *admiratio*, he allows himself the role of partisan of self-display because, in a corrupt and dangerous world, dissimulation, masks, and all manner of strategies that conceal and disguise are virtues for the prudent man, "el discreto."

Góngora is less inclined to compromise with the critics of ostentation, and in his sponsorship of the peacock – of the autonomy, buoyancy, and transforming power of the imagination – he can be claimed as a forerunner of Wallace Stevens. Stevens, in his second draft of "A Collect of Philosophy," paints the following scene as a summary of his thoughts concerning the relations between poetry and philosophy:

> There comes into the mind a procession of a great crowd of men, a little bent over as if they were scholars. They are holding on, by ceremonial ropes, to a kind of floor in the air, which they are conducting, or better, attending in its progress. As is natural to an aerial floor, in rhetoric, it is made of ivory. On it, and at its center, there is a blue peacock, blue and green and all the denser modulations of these colors, with gold and silver fans, which it turns to and fro as if to exhibit the brilliance of its mere presence and thereby to command. On the peacock's head, there is a diamond crown, like a coxcomb of darting light and darting fire. As this image of imagination passes us, we are impressed by the manner of its attendant persons, alien and obedient, as if they were grateful for some expectation of their labor, of which they seem to feel sure. (*Wallace Stevens* 55)

This resplendent and superbly gongorine totem of reverential scholars somehow floats on an ivory carpet, gliding slowly and ceremoniously, in keeping with the mystique of its royal persona, its aura of command. An emblem of the "gaiety of language," it operates improbably as an aerial anchor, fastening the philosopher-scholars to a spectacle which possesses both buoyancy and mineral density.

Góngora's peacock, no less magisterial, appears in Stanza 13 of the *Polifemo* as a Venusian creature, for it is framed within the transposition in which Venus and Juno exchange emblematic birds:

> pavón de Venus es, cisne de Juno.[2]

---

[2] All quotations from the *'Polifemo'* will be from Dámaso Alonso, *Góngora y 'El Polifemo.'* Verse translations from the *Polifemo* are by Gilbert F. Cunningham, from A. A. Parker's *'Polyphemus and Galatea: A Study in the Interpretation of a Baroque Poem;* prose translations are my own.

The fusion of the two birds in the last lines of the stanza completes the earlier figure which presents Galatea in terms of the luminous eyes which adorn her white plumage:

> Son una y otra luminosa estrella
> lucientes ojos de su blanca pluma

[One and another luminous star, the bright eyes of her white plumage.]

The swan has acquired the "eyes" of the peacock, while the peacock takes on the gliding quality of the swan through its attachment to Venus, and is absorbed into the luminous whiteness of the scene, into light itself.

In Stanza 46 the Cyclops initiates his song by re-stating the poet's earlier comparison of Galatea to swan and peacock, drawing attention again to the multiple-eyed plumage of the peacock, now enhanced by the addition of the color blue, a blue "field" arranged for the device of the eye-stars:

> igual en pompa al pájaro que, grave
> su manto azul de tantos ojos dora
> cuantas el celestial zafiro estrellas:
>
> (365-68)

[As majestic as the stately bird who adorns his blue cloak with as many eyes as there are stars in the celestial sapphire]

Sky and sea in Góngora's lexicon are frequently designated by the same vehicle – "zafiro" – and each is a figured expanse of blueness against which some luminous even may take place: the convergence of solar and lunar light in the constellation Taurus in the *Soledades*, the efflorescence of divinity in the *Polifemo*. In the *Polifemo* the sea generates *espuma*, white spume which is, like the peacock, a figure of gratuitous self-display, and, as I will make clear in Chapter III, this "kingdom of sea-spume" is for Góngora an image of the locus of aesthetic activity.

Gongorismo, like Stevens's aerial peacock, attended rather than led by his procession of scholars, does not point beyond itself. Instead, like the pilgrim protagonist of the *Soledades* rather than the pupil of Gracián's sage, the reader is led not forward towards an "edad varonil" of manly and sober maturity, but astray into delinquency by the errant and exfoliant paths of the poem. In the *Soledad Primera* the poet and his shipwrecked pilgrim set out on a solitary and uncertain path, bereft of guiding doctrine and transcendental goal:

> Pasos de un peregrino son errante
> cuantos me dictó dulce musa
>   en soledad confusa
> perdidos unos, otros inspirados.
>
> [Dictated by the Muse, these verses, know,
> as many footsteps as the pilgrim made;
> though some in solitude confused have strayed
> others inspired were born.][3]

While the path taken by the poet and his reader appears to be less spiritual and strenuous than that of Gracián's travellers, it is at the same time the more meditative journey. The country path or road is a metaphor for Being in the thought of Heidegger:

> It is said about these that they are overgrown because they are rarely trodden, and that they end suddenly in tracklessness. Man can get lost on them. They themselves get lost, however in one and the same forest of one in the same Being. (Vycinas 113)

It can also stand for the thinking that responds to Being:

> As a response, thinking of Being is a highly errant and in addition a very destitute matter. Thinking is perhaps, after all, an unavoidable path, which refuses to be a path of salvation and brings no new wisdom (*Poetry* 185)

The oblique and meditative "movimiento hacia afuera" of *gongorismo*, its attentive regard for the multiple, swerves away from the straight path, and this is the core of its essential radicalism and of its buoyancy. The peacock which becomes like a swan, or sea-

---

[3] *The Solitudes*. Translation by Edward Meryon Wilson (20). Subsequent quotations from the *Soledades* will be from this edition.

spume, which in turn is a nymph playing like light over the surface of the water, is *buoyed up*. In Góngora's system of meaning, as we will see, singularity is equivalent to depth and gravity (monotheism), while multiplicity is surface and levity (polytheism). The imagination is at home on the surface, mistrustful of saturnine depths.

The pluralism which is such an important feature of *gongorismo* is simply the natural polytheism of the poet; like Yeats, Góngora adheres to a "plurality of worship" (Vendler 104), for only multiple divinity can satisfy the imagination: "The only divinity imagination can acknowledge is Proteus" (104). For Quevedo, a militant monotheist, the world is invariably weighed down by the subject which confronts it, and is eventually reduced to ashes and dust, along with the desiring ego. The things of the world collapse into a reminder of death, the great leveller of forms:

> Y no hallé cosa en que poner los ojos
> que no fuese recuerdo de la muerte.
> (Salmos XVIII)
>
> [and I found nothing to set eyes upon
> that was not a reminder of death]

In one of his many tracts, in this case in defense of the monarchy, Quevedo asserts that "Oneness is a prime principle in nature." (Bleznick 140) It is scarcely surprising that the *conceptista* poet would feel no attraction to the hundred-eyed bird, and that he would compare his rival disparagingly to the painter Bosch. (Collard 24.n.73)

The new style in Flemish painting, interestingly enough, seems to have been a source of irritation to more than one Spanish scholar, for much the same reasons that the new style in poetry caused unease. The Abad de Rute, otherwise an apologist for Góngora, compared Góngora's attention to detail and his habit of "burying" the central idea beneath a heavily embroidered surface of imagery to a Flemish painting in which

> se veen industriosa y hermosíssimamente pintados mil géneros de exercicios rústicos, cacerías, chozas, montes, valles, prados, bosques, mares, esteros, ríos, arroyos, animales terrestres, aquáticos y aéreos. (Collard 83)

[One sees, carefully and beautifully painted, a thousand kinds of rustic details, hunting parties, cottages, mountains, valleys, meadows, woods seas, marshes, rivers, brooks, terrestrial, aquatic and aerial animals.]

A similar assessment of the disturbingly diffuse effects of Flemish painting is made by Father Bernardino de Villegas, who complains that in a scene supposedly depicting Saint Jerome, almost the entire canvas is monopolized by the various elements of landscape: birds, animals, groves, rivers, etc., and only in a corner do we discern the figure of the penitent saint, meekly occupying a space "the size of a thumb." (Collard 83) In both painting and poetry, what was formerly relegated to the background has now advanced to the foreground, and man himself seems to have been demoted and de-centered, made secondary to the fascination with the "light in things" – to the phenomenal context of which man thought himself to be the focal point and "arbiter."

While this attraction to the outward forms of things is a prominent feature of *culteranismo*, it coexists with metaphors typical of the more centripetal *conceptismo* which, like those of metaphysical poetry, depend for effect more upon the reader's apprehension of an abstract equivalence than a physical resemblance. In the tenth stanza of the *Polifemo* the straw in which the pear rests is a "pale tutor" or guardian:

> la pera, de quien fue cuna dorada
> la rubia paja y –pálida tutora–,
> la niega avara y pródiga la dora.
> (78-80)

[the pear, of whom the yellow straw was the gilded bed and, as a pale tutor, it greedily hoards and prodigally gilds.]

The straw – "la rubia paja," which coyly displays and conceals its charge – ensures its ripening: the simultaneous display and concealment are typical of Góngora's sometimes teasing style of presentation. And though the golden aura of the figure is insistent, it is the function of *tutor* or *duenna* and not a visual resemblance which underpins the unexpected comparison.

Alonso cites lines 213-14 in the *Polifemo* as evidence that audacious fusions of things apparently disparate are not the exclusive property of *conceptismo*:

> Vagas cortinas de volantes vanos
> corrió Favonio...

The lines compare the breeze, rising to wake Galatea, to curtains which are pulled open to arouse the sleeper. But note that the comparison is not an entirely conceptual one such as we might find in John Donne; rather the reader is made aware of a sensation, through the repeated v's, as though air brushing against the face were given a slight weight of some soft fabric. And we are moved to note that, as in the first passage cited, the conceit or abstract comparison is employed as an enhancement to sensuous mood or event; in the first example we are given a witty still-life scene: the pear and straw are anthropomorphized so that the idea straw: tutor; pear: pupil adds an invisible dimension to the phenomena presented: the golden surface of the ripening fruit resting in its yellow bed of straw.

The abstraction which is already performed by still-life painting on the first level of representation – the thing detached from its natural surroundings and placed in an artistic grouping – is here refined and complicated by a further abstraction to a second level not available to the painter. The turn of wit ripples the surface of the painted scene as the mind turns inward to consider the comparison, and then subsides as the images of apple, pear, and acorn recompose themselves as the fruits of the Sicilian harvest claimed by Polyphemus. The "hypocritical apple" of the same passage "deceives," in a witty inversion of the falsely pure countenance, by concealing its candid interior under a florid complexion:

> ... la manzana hipócrita, que engaña,
> a lo pálido no, a lo arrebolado,

[the hypocritical apple, who deceives not by pallor but by paint]

The sensuous appeal of these and similar figures is well known, as are the complex patterns and formulas of the poet's wit; the recognition of the latter has accorded him some measure of intellectual respectability.[4] But while the ornamental and the conceptual invariably overlap in *gongorismo*, it is the ornate noun with its entourage of modifiers which claims supremacy in the grammatical hierarchy: "espumoso mar," "caverna profunda," "rubia paja," "bárbaro ruido," "luminosa estrella," "fiero jayán ciego," "horrenda voz"; even more than the things themselves, it is their *qualities* which claim to be exclusive centers of meaning: the foaminess of the Sicilian sea, the depth and darkness of the cavern, the whiteness of the nymph, the horror of Polyphemus's voice, the silver of Acis's transformed blood. The prominence of these adjectives, beings in their own right, calls to mind Frank Kermode's remark of Wallace Stevens, that the making of poetry, for Stevens, is "to bring the great adjective of the poem to this primordial noun" which is reality. (98)

Gracián, anticipating Antonio Machado's criticism of Góngora, is suspicious of the poet's web of substantives, and asserts as a corrective the primacy of the verb, the "nerve" of literary style. The verb should be taut, tense, magnetic:

> Mas el nervio del estilo consiste en la intensa profundidad del verbo.... Preñado ha de ser el verbo, no hinchado, que signifique, que no resuene: verbos con fondo, donde se engolfe la atención, donde tenga en que cebarse la comprensión (*Agudeza* 234)
>
> [But the nerve of style consists in the intense profundity of the verb.... It should be compressed, not swollen; let it signify without resounding; verbs with depth and substance, where the attention of the reader is engulfed, where understanding can fasten itself.

Notice that while Góngora wants to lead the reader astray, to entangle us with his complex and witty presentation of images, Gracián wants to pull the reader down into meaning by means of a vortex of verbs. The reader is both active and passive in relation to the verb, engulfed by its "fondo" (bottom, floor, ground, essence), but able to cast anchor somewhere beneath the surface of

---

[4] For a summary of the tradition of wit and the issue of *conceptismo* in Góngora, see A. A. Parker, op. cit.

discourse. The reader assumes the role of a Persephone, strolling in a flowery meadow and suddenly seized by Hades; unaware, she stumbles into the cave of *logos*, the deep place concealed by a flowering meadow of rhetoric.

Góngora's "objectivist" style in some respects looks forward to the Imagist movement and to the scrupulous requirement of poetry that it extinguish the personality of the poet while attending to the thing "in itself."[5] Góngora's adjectival embroidery would surely have invited Pound's scything, for the latter wanted, at least for a time, "straight talk" from poetry and the baroque Andalusian is the master of the most exquisite of circumlocutions. But Góngora nonetheless, like the Imagists, worked towards the liberation of the image, in fusion with sound, from concept, anecdote, and personal feeling. Paul Julian Smith observes of Góngora's poetry that it provides a model for Barthes' idea of a textual utopia, in which the paradigms of orthodoxy are eluded, and meaning becomes the "object of free play." The ecstatic text, for Barthes was the "gongorine" text; textual pleasure

> sets up in the heart of (current) human relations a sort of island, manifests the asocial nature of pleasure (only leisure is social), makes us glimpse the scandalous truth of rapture: that it could well be (if all linguistic imaginary is abolished) *neuter*. (Smith 90)

Gongorine textures (texture: a compromise which removes the possibility of absolute depth or absolute surface) are the province of Venus, who dissolves the pretended solidity of self into its appearance, and into its helpless response to appearance. Meaning resides only within this utopia of entangling nouns and qualities "Le substantif, dans sa majesté sustantielle, l'adjectif, vêtement transparent qui l'habille et le colore comme un glacis..." (Baudelaire 376).

It is precisely the attention given to the alluring substantive, key to the "esprit paradisiaque," which seemed to Antonio Macha-

---

[5] Michel Serres speculates on the implications of an attentiveness to the object: "... it makes an opening and something like a chance to escape from the network of our relations, and therefore, to free us from the problems posed by this network, in particular, the problem of violence. What pertains to the object will perhaps be neutral terrain." (*Hermes* 123)

do to disqualify Góngora from the ranks of serious poetry. To Machado baroque poetry itself was irretrievably decadent – its ornate language had "fallen" from a state of pure and spontaneous expression which is the poetic state of grace. Poetry was for Machado above all a temporal art which properly expressed the "psychic movement" of the poet through intuitive images. Góngora's imagery, he claims, rarely escapes the tired formulations of his inherited renaissance lexicon; it is conceptual rather than intuitive, schematic to the point that it takes on the frozen aspect of a syllogism. This category of imagery, Machado insists, originates outside the authentic psychic time of the poet and merely serves to express, disguise, or decorate concepts. (345)

I cite Machado as representative of the most cogent of Góngora's more recent detractors, and because his criticism focuses on the nature of Góngora's evocative imagery and grammar, a crucial issue in my own study. It is the illusion of a cessation of movement which troubles Machado; this, and an unrelenting intellectualism which precludes the primary operation of poetic activity which is to provide singular images which convey the intuitive movements of the poet's psyche. Images have no business consorting with abstract concepts; in so doing they betray their primary bond with intuition. For Machado this illicit union of image and concept results in verse which is a series of "emarañados laberintos verbales," "tangled verbal labyrinths" (344-45) which offend as much by their florid, unpruned growth as by their arid pedantry. Machado sums up his critique with a statement about the universal concern of artistic creation, declaring that true creativity concerns itself exclusively with "essential 'man'" which the poet discerns in himself and presupposes in others.

Let us now consider the issue of "gravity," of so much concern to seventeenth century detractors, against the background of Machado's anthropomorphic view of the world addressed by poetic discourse. Gravity is a demeanor and a property of discourse aligned with the moral and metaphysical concerns of man. It is not manifest in the plumage of the peacock, which is, on the contrary, a symbol of levitation and even of levity. Nor does it reside in the "light in things" which invites imaginative and speculative response. It is attached to a kind of humanism and a concern with "essential man" which is implied, for example, in Michelangelo's objections to the new genre of landscape painting which was coming into vogue in the late renaissance. (The pre-eminence of painting among the arts of the seventeenth century is at least in part due to the reinforcement it drew from the landscape genre itself, for the new genre freed the medium from the sculptural style of the renaissance. [Friedlander 19, 20]) Michelangelo quite logically despised the landscape, for it diverted attention from underlying, eternal structures to the transient textures of natural world. It took delight in "stuffs," – "bricks and mortar, the grass of the fields, the shadows of trees, and bridges and rivers, which they call landskips, and little figures here and there..." (Clark 54).

What seems to be a kind of nihilism when judged from the viewpoint of this kind of essentialism is in face evidence of a profound shift in focus in seventeenth century poetry as well as painting. This turning towards the context within which human beings exist (occurring, ironically, at the dawn of the technological age) is at the same time a reflection on the nature of the media of representation, the capacities of words and images for bringing to light worlds and things without the mediation of inherited definitions. In this "turning" Góngora demonstrates his affinity with the northern painters and their concern with the qualities of space within which human history unfolds. His poesis performs the paradoxical task of employing a set of conventions inherited from the renaissance in such a way that it destroys itself as a grid through which to view the world. The world is seen to elude – as Galatea eludes her giant suitor – the grid of language, and we are left only with – language. But because of this deliberate cleavage, by which the grid becomes as opaque as a map to a legendary country, the world, like the sky in a Dutch landscape, acquires a disquieting presence formerly denied it. Because of an extraordinarily acute consciousness of his materials, Góngora was able to bend them to serve his own unique vision of the world. This vision does not, as Machado claims, turn its back on nature but, like the new genres of landscape and still-life, works towards disclosing the forms and hidden patterns of nature as it discloses its own operations as poetic thinking.

The issue, then, of materialization and quantification, still troublesome to some modern readers, may be approached with more insight if we are able to set aside and examine what amounts to a modern bias towards not only the invisible movements of intuition but also energy in its opposition to and even annihilation of form and matter. Energy itself is our center of gravity, and we honor, like Machado and Gracián, the verb rather than the noun, tending to see meaning in actions rather than in things and their qualities. Góngora's aberrant language of values frequently places the subjects of verbs in danger of being beside the point, as in the first stanza of the Dedication to the *Polifemo*:

> Estas que me dictó rimas sonoras,
> cultas sí, aunque bucólica, Talía

[These sonorous rhymes, dictated to me by the learned, though rustic Thalia]

Muse and poet, collaborators in sonorous and learned verse, are subject and object to an act — inspiration — but the act itself is subordinate to the *sonority* of the verses as well as to the muse's bucolic and learned nature.

The privileged placement of sonority directly violates Gracián's requirement for serious discourse, which is that it *signify without* the distraction of sonority. It is the qualities which assert themselves here: sonorous, learned, bucolic — and announce the style of the poem which is about to unfold. The entire pattern of the stanza will reinforce this emphasis — it is the sonority of the pipes which is crucial, not Thalia, not the invoked listener, the patron, or even the poet. It is the inhumanness of sound which, floating free of human concerns, surrounds and links the other identities of the passage. The second half of the stanza rises to the imperative "Escucha, al son de la zampoña mía," a command which will be echoed by the Cyclops in his song to Galatea: ". . . escucha un día mi voz, por dulce, cuando no por mía." (383-84) In this same line the earlier "sonoras" ripples across the "field" of the verse, reverberating in "son" and "zampoña," the sound of the shepherd-poet's pipes. The submersion of subject and verb in a field of qualities will be used to greatest effect in Stanza 13 (see Chapter II), upon which the entire issue of Cyclopean song could be said to turn.

Góngora's "objectivism," then, consists in the fact that meaning tends to inhabit *objects* rather than *subjects* — though the subject/object formula can already be seen to be inadequate to the relations it is called upon to describe. Substance resides in the world, to which the self is in thrall, even when it pretends or aspires to control and pre-eminence. The ego's interpretive seizures tend to be effaced or muted in a cosmos of displayed appearances. Even Polyphemus, the poem's symbolic subjectivity, and the closest we ever get to Góngora's own guarded inwardness, is immersed in and seems almost immobilized by the qualities which define him: it is impossible to dislodge him as an acting subject from these qualities, many of which fuse him with his landscape: the cave dwelling precedes his delineation, a "melancholy void" whose metaphors and modifiers dominate three stanzas; then his own appearance: the mountainous stature (l. 49); the solar eye (51-52); the great heavy shepherd's staff, compared to a pine tree (53-54); the Lethean torrent of wavy black hair; the towering cliff on which he stands to deliver his song.

At the pictorial center of the poem are the two contrasting images of Cyclops and nymph, a tense unity of two irreconcilable states of being: one, monstrosity, is in itself a negation of beauty, even as it lurches after it in the guise of an amorous giant; the other, ideal beauty, is in perpetual flight from the monstrous. In the interaction of these two figures we find a key to the baroque ambivalence to inherited forms, the tension between its tendencies towards idolatry and iconoclasm. For both these figures are so positioned in Góngora's revision of the tale that each makes a strong claim to defining the world: Cyclopean monstrosity is the reality of a devouring subjectivity, while the nymph inhabits a paradise of forms which negates the formless inwardness of monstrosity. For Gracián the realm of forms in nature is merely the threshold through which we are exhorted to pass to the realm of the ethical, "la edad varonil," the "virile age" which succeeds the puerile sense-entanglements of youth. Once we reside there, as securely installed as the sage who is beyond the lure of the feminine "Falsirena," the beauties of the world are relegated to the status of *engaño*, illusion and deceit. We are encouraged to join the ranks of the prudent, the disillusioned ones for whom melancholy disillusion, *desengaño*, is a state of enlightenment, a release from the bondage of the world and its myriad entrapments.

Gongorismo, conversely, seeks immersion in *engaño*, for illusion and enchantment are remedies for that very melancholy which the sage embraces as the emotional condition for his moral salvation.

It trumpets, with Stevens, the "gaiety of language." The two long poems which have come to define *gongorismo* mark the height of the poet's creative powers, his capacity to oppose to what Stevens called the "violence from without," or "the pressure of reality," the violence from within which is for Stevens the essence of a radically subversive "nobility" (*Necessary Angel* 36). By the formal deployment of his personality, its characteristic tensions and emphases, Góngora enacts the "turning away" which underpins a radically aristocratic form-world whose every verse incorporates disdain — disdain as the principle of *selection*, negation, indifference to the near, the accessible, the accurate.

Hector Ciocchini remarks of the hard, lapidary lights of Góngora's imagery that there is a causal relationship between anguish and exquisite formalism:

> Las obras de belleza equilibrada y rara perfección son obras de los desesperados que hallan la salvación momentánea en un orden expresivo, en una provisoria claridad que mitigue las crecientes olas de sombra de su existencia. (10)

> [Works of measured beauty and rare perfection are works of the desperate, who seek momentary salvation in an expressive order, in a provisional clarity which mitigates the growing waves of shadows in their lives.]

The hard lights of formal perfection are set against the everincreasing darkness of the poet's historical existence. *Gongorismo*, as will become clear in the following chapters, is the aesthetic response to melancholy, a means by which one may avoid the awakening to barren truth (for the will-to-truth, as Nietzsche would later remark, may in fact be a disguised will-to-death). (*The Gay Science* 282) The will to illusion, as the cultivation of the *via aesthetica*, views the insistence upon the unadorned truth of the *via ascetica* as a forlorn state of existence, a soulless cave-dwelling barren of the snares of images, of the beguilement of light, color and form.

Góngora's opponents, the party of the "iglesia Castellana," regarded his verse as "pestilential," "fraudulent," and "delirious." More to the point, they hinted at moral vacuity, heresy, and even atheism. (Collard, "herejía" 32) The view that *gongorismo* constituted an "infernal secta," a heretical challenge to literary orthodoxy, is not rooted exclusively in a distaste for a hyperbolic style of poetry weighted down with excessive word-play, latinisms and syntactic distortions. For underlying these formal objections to what was perceived to be confusion, perversion, and dislocation (the same charges were made against the Roman baroque architect Borromini, for many of the same reasons) is the recognition of a radical inversion of values, nothing less than the turning of Western metaphysics on its head. For *culteranismo*, finally more radical in its implications than *luteranismo*, proposes, first, that there is no reality other than what appears. To be undisclosed, lacking visibility, is to verge on the monstrous and to be deprived of a place in the order of things, the paradise of forms, of Being itself. While his contemporaries Quevedo and Gracián were frequently occupied with exposing, by means of satire and allegory, the world of baroque Spain as a grotesque puppet show of hollow theatrical gestures (one thinks especially of Quevedo's *El Buscón*, an exercise in provoking revulsion from the physical world) Góngora's long poems propose a vision of nature which challenges the claim of court and society, with its human distortions and duplicities, to be a world at all. They propose a transference of value to *rerum natura*, to a world "ensouled," to borrow James Hillman's phrase. ("Anima Mundi" 93)

A second premise of *gongorismo*, which will be explored more fully in succeeding chapters, is that a perceiving subject (Cyclops) may not plausibly claim primacy over the world it inhabits and contemplates. The Cyclopean claim to supremacy in the world is one meaning of the monstrous: a mode of perception which seizes upon and devours reality, assimilating it to a single perspective.

In considering the task of the poet as first of all that of bringing forth phenomena into the light of the poem we may recall that Lucretius invoked Venus as the goddess of universal disclosure, of *rerum natura*, of all things in their coming-into-being in the light. Vycinas writes that every god is a world and a reality in itself, in the sense of a specific mode in which the natural world appears. Each provides the *logos* for *physis*, disclosing an essence of nature. (218-223) Aphrodite brings forth the charm and allure of nature, the "reino de la espuma" which is the sea as it gleams in the sunlight, as well as the flowering meadows, shady groves and bowers, and human beauty. For Góngora, as for Lucretius, Venus rules the spectacle and the unfolding of the visible world, and "sums up" its beauties as she shines through the figure of Galatea: "... dulce en ella / el terno Venus de sus Gracias suma" [In her are sweetly enfolded the Graces of the tender Venus] (99-100). She is the focus of the color and the light of the world, its grace of images. Her essence is revealed in Galatea, who, as a synecdoche for the goddess, is one mode of appearance of the divine, of the power of love and beauty. The realm of the Venusian Galatea, the "reino de la espuma," is the realm of aesthetic creation, a depth which casts up shining surfaces. As we will see in Chapter III, the Cyclops functions at one level in the poem as a perspective – a singular and reductive way of confronting the appearing world. In this respect, as in others, the giant shepherd reveals himself as a Saturnine type, devouring and hoarding, irrevocably removed from Schopenhauer's "will-less enjoyment of the translucent." (375) The Cyclopean perception of images is never without intention, and more often than not is an attempt at seizure: images solidify, become objects, dragged into the darkness of the cave-vault. In this sense Polyphemus – sullen, colossal, engorged – is the titanic antithesis to all meditative thinking and to the aesthetic response to the world – despite the fact that for a brief time he is a poet. The world in its resplendency threatens to vanish under the heavy, Cyclopean gaze, becoming "fugitiva" like the nymph who eludes him.

But despite this antithesis of monstrosity and beauty at the core of the poem – the *chiaroscuro* play of devouring subject and elusive appearance which provides the impetus for the poem's unfolding mythos – the baroque Cyclops in his melancholy awareness of his own deprivation points to a submerged aspect of aestheticism itself. And it is this very consciousness of the discrepancy between the self, man-as-abyss, and the radiant world which the artist seeks to disclose, which provides the current of melancholy we find running through Góngora's poetry, and which surfaces in the patches of darkness in such sonnets as "De un caminante enfermo" (1594), "Cosas, Celalba mía, he visto" (1596); in the delicate nihilism of the *letrilla* "Alegoría de la brevedad de las cosas humanas" (1621); and in the sudden extinction of palace lights in the "Panegírico al Duque de Lerma" (1617).

But it is in the *Polifemo* that the poet formulates, in his Cyclops, a major symbol for his own estrangement from and adoration of the Venusian realm of beauty, and for the human condition itself in its helpless yearning towards a reality which seems both to lure and to exclude, to invite possession and to perpetually elude even the attempts of language to seize and contain it. The Cyclops figure testifies to the remoteness of paradise in a poem which aspires to be a linguistic reconstruction of paradise.

2. THE CYCLOPS AND HIS CLASSICAL LINEAGE

Of the three figures who compose the ancient love triangle in Góngora's poem it is Polyphemus who carries the greatest weight of literary and mythological associations. Coming upon this figure, we are immediately drawn to look beyond his present literary incarnation, first to his antecedents in Ovid, Theocritus, Homer, Hesiod, and then to the larger family of ogres and giants in mythology and folklore.[6] By reason of his imposing lineage, and by the tradition of his monstrous appearance and savage behavior, Polyphemus is excluded from the poetic territory designated by Stevens's "floating ivory floor." Unlike the elusive Galatea, an airy compound of light, foam, plumage, crystal, and the crimson of Platonic carnations, Polyphemus, as we will see, is a center of gravity in the poem. It is this threat of an absolute centripetal force which is precisely the threat that subjectivism poses to poetry. The struggle between the two yields the oxymoronic Cyclopean song – a vast dissonance which is a lyrical prelude to violence.

The earliest Greek formulation of the Polyphemus who will appear as the rejected and murderous lover of Ovid's tale exploited the comic potential (the ogre is never far from the buffoon) latent in the still earlier Homeric episode. Philoxenus of Cythera (d. 370/ 379 b.c.) features the giant as a loutish suitor in a dithyramb which satirizes Dionisius, the ruler of Syracuse, thus initiating the pastoral deflation of the epic giant. A parallel tradition originates in Sicilian folklore, which provides the story of the love triangle and the Cyclops's murder of his rival Acis, whose blood becomes the river of the same name. In Theocritus's *Idyls* 11 and 30 we find

---

[6] The most detailed study of classical sources and themes in the *Polifemo* is Antonio Vilanova's *Las fuentes y los temas del 'Polifemo' de Góngora*. See also Robert Jammes, and Dámaso Alonso, *Góngora y el 'Polifemo'* I. 9 for concise overviews of the subject.

the Cyclops still pining for his nymph and by the time Ovid takes his turn with the story Polyphemus has become a stock pastoral type, groping his way towards a kind of rustic civility, a reformed cannibal preening himself, Narcissus-like, before a pool.

While we are chiefly concerned with the Cyclops as a figure of pastoral, Ovid's tale and its subsequent renaissance variants cannot fail to remind the reader of an earlier tradition in which the Cyclops's primitive habit of violence is unrelated to thwarted amorous yearnings. The very incongruity of the pastoral Cyclops in his surroundings, the immense dissonance caused by his savage solitude, crude pride in ownership and murderous jealousy, point to this earlier tradition which links him to titanic, underworld powers. He is also associated, paradoxically, with the triumph of the Olympian deities over the powers of earth and darkness, for he shifts allegiance to the gods of the upper world. In Hesiod's *Theogony* the Cyclops unfolds into the three one-eyed sons of Gaia and Ouranos, who play a key role in the evolution of the idea of deity from elemental forces to the anthropomorphic pantheon with its reigning sky-god Zeus. The alliance of the Cyclopes with Zeus in his war against the Titans releases them from subterranean imprisonment: having been cast into a dungeon by a jealous father, they are subsequently released by a shrewder nephew: Zeus, son of Cronus, who consolidates his position as sky-god through his decisive defeat of the chthonic Titans. In gratitude the Cyclopes provide the crucial weapons, thunderbolts and lightning, for his victory. The battle reaches a peak of intensity as Zeus brings in his fiery Cyclopean weaponry:

> Then Zeus decided to restrain his own power no longer. A sudden surge of energy filled his spirit, and he exerted all the strength he had. He advance through the sky from Olympus sending flash upon flash of continuous lightning. The bolts of lightning and thunder flew thick and fast from his powerful arm, forming a solid roll of sacred fire. (Brown 72)

The Titans are blinded by the violent light, and the heat of the fire suffocates them in their underground stronghold.

From this source in Hesiod springs the tradition of the Cyclopes as gold-rivaling artisans. And yet Virgil will later compare them, in *The Georgics,* to industrious bees – programmed and unimaginative functionaries who will serve in the *Aeneid* as Vulcan's workmen, the "brotherhood of Aetna," in his underground forge. (*Georgics* 167-76; *Aeneid* III)

Homer's Polyphemus, in contrast to the elemental arms suppliers in Hesiod and Virgil, is endowed with a forceful individuality, perhaps in order to provide a sufficiently impressive adversary for the epic hero. In Book IX of *The Odyssey* the giant cannibal who is blinded by Odysseus and whose prayer to Poseidon impedes the hero's journey home arrogantly claims a god-like autonomy. Now a cave-dwelling shepherd rather than a forge worker, he quickly disabuses Odysseus of any expectations of a divinely sanctioned hospitality, and flaunts his disrespect for Olympus:

> Stranger, you are a simple fool, or come from far off,
> when you tell me to avoid the wrath of the gods or fear them:
> The Cyclopes do not concern themselves over Zeus of the aegis,
> nor any of the rest of the blessed gods, since we are far better
> than they, and for fear of Zeus I would not spare
> you or your companions either, if the fancy took me otherwise.
>   (273-279)

Like the suitors who are besieging Penelope in Ithaka the Cyclopes neither fear the gods nor pity their victims. Polyphemus lives and kills only for himself, and is only very loosely attached to a tribe of similarly lawless shepherds, his brother-Cyclopes who fail to decipher and heed his cry that "nobody" has maimed him. The members of this exclusively and vehemently masculine society are wholly self-sufficient, or appear to be, each ruling his own territory consisting of a cave and surrounding mountain pastures. In his depiction of Polyphemus Homer presents us with a kind of anti-social *übermensch*, confident of his omnipotence until he is forced by his maiming to call upon the avenging power of his father Poseidon. And here he seems not entirely confident of his paternity: his identity slips, for he has been disabled by "Nobody," who sails off taunting his victim with psychological missiles:

> Cyclops, if any mortal man ever asks you who it was
> that inflicted upon your eye this shameful blinding,

Tell him that you were blinded by Odysseus, sacker of cities;
Laertes is his father, and he makes his home in Ithaka.
                                                    (502-05)

The blinded and defeated giant invokes his own paternal magic, calling to Poseidon with upraised arms:

Hear me, Poseidon who circles the earth, dark-haired. If truly
I am your son, and you acknowledge yourself as my father
Grant that Odysseus, sacker of cities, son of Laertes,
Who makes his home in Ithaka, may never reach that home;
                                                    (528-30)

The travails which issue from this curse end only with Odysseus' rescue by the hospitable Phaiakians, former neighbors to the Cyclopes, and now an eager and appreciative audience to the hero's narration of his misfortunes.

W. F. Knight persuasively argues that the epic Cyclopes, outwitted by a shrewder adversary, is a relic of the stone age, defeated by the superior *technē* of a later and more sophisticated culture. In Book VI of the *Aeneid* the stone walls which encircle Elysium are reported to have been constructed by the Cyclopes, and Knight observes that these "ring walls" were an attribute, along with caves, labyrinths and underground dwellings, of the megalithic era. Thus the Cyclops is the stone age man who built circular or "cyclopean" walls; and there is an archaeological as well as mythological basis for the motifs of circumscription and defensive symbolism which surround Gongora's lovesick giant. It will suffice as an anthropological aside to quote Knight's summary: "A Cyclops is a man, who by the action of legendary wonder has grown to be more than a man, and who builds Cyclopean walls, and makes or uses caves under the earth." (169)

The subterranean site is a forge in the Hesiodic tradition, and in Virgil the Cyclopes as weapons makers to Zeus acquire a supervisor in Vulcan, the god of fire. The one-eyed giants are no longer inventors, but assistants, appearing in Book III of *The Aeneid* as the "brotherhood of Aetna." The Trojans arrive at a Sicilian harbor with Mt. Aetna looming in the background, and the mountain's vomit of boulders and smoke and flame is attributed to the stirrings of the buried giant Enceladus (1. 578) Achamenides, a ragged survivor of Odysseus's Sicilian expedition, appears, and his account of the monster transposes the menacing attributes of Enceladus/Aetna to the huge and hideous Cyclops: his enormous height, like the flames from the volcano, disturbs the very stars; his ghastly vomiting of flesh and wine echoes the earlier description of volcanic eruptions, and the bellowing voice roars and rumbles through the caves under the mountain.

The gloom and violence of Virgil's extended metaphor inform the volcanic locale of Gongora's opening stanzas, whose primary features are height and subterranean depth. The poet concentrates the giant/volcano metaphor into a single line: "un monte era de miembros eminente." (49) The horrendous bellowing of his voice (St. 61), compared to the warning thunder before a storm, precedes his murder of Acis and completes the figure of the giant as a focus of telluric and meteorological forces.

It is the mountain fortress rather than the subterranean cave that fascinated Plato and provided a mythical locale for his own notion of an archetypal polity in *Laws* III. It is interesting that the philosopher offers a somewhat nostalgic view of the same primitivism which supplied a fearful adversary for Odysseus and comic material for pastoral poets. The very traits which make Homer's tribe of giant shepherds a type of monstrous exception to the customs and codes of both the Homeric and pastoral worlds are evidence to Plato of their freedom from corruption. For while these creatures are elsewhere in literature depicted as conspicuously and hopelessly savage, the "Athenian" extols their primitive condition as a kind of innocence; their rudeness, rather than an outrage to standards of civility, can be viewed as virtuous simplicity – a notion not far from the more sentimental idea of the "noble savage." While these communities of ideal rustics, arising after the cataclysmic flood, are acknowledged as primitive, impoverished, and highly defensive tribal confederations, their lack of technical sophistication is seen as a credit. (118-124) They are uncorrupted, viewed from the perspective of supposed cultural decline. Moreover they serve as early and not entirely undesirable models, for Plato, of patriarchal rule.

We need to pause and consider certain features of Plato's myth more closely, since they are pertinent to our grasp of the baroque Cyclops and the patterns of his strange singularity. First, the political nostalgia expressed in *Laws* III for a Golden Age of autocracy casts the Cyclops in a role very similar to that of the Roman god Saturn. For while Saturn, when conflated with the Greek Cronus, is the savage patriarch who, after castrating his father Uranus, devours his own children, he is also imagined to have reigned over the peaceful Golden Age as an agricultural god. Before he was defeated by his son Zeus and cast into the underworld, he presided over an age which needed no laws, navigation, wars, mining, plows, or butchers. In Góngora's poem this Mediterranean paradise is "candor primero," primal candor or innocence. (l. 88) Ovid writes in *Metamorphoses* I: ". . . The Golden Age was first, a time that cherished / Of its own will, justice / and right"; (88-89) and "Spring was forever, with a west wind blowing / Softly across the flowers no man had planted, . . ." (106-07). Like Saturn/Cronus Polyphemus is, in fact, both pastoral and anti-pastoral, and the key to this contradictory role lies in his Saturnine nature, a feature of his identity I will address in Chapter II.

Second, we must consider the significance of the initial adversarial relation of Plato's Cyclops to the sea: Cyclopean society is founded *in reaction to* the flood and as a barrier between organized human existence (culture) and the destructive power of water (elemental nature). Plato's post-diluvian man erects his primitive culture, logically, as an *opus contra naturam*, in opposition to inundation and dissolution. The withdrawal to a high place, then, is the primary organizing device of Cyclopean culture and is decisive to the shaping of a character type which will receive its fullest representation in the baroque.[7]

This highly relevant gesture of withdrawal and fortification in Plato's mythical polity clearly resembles the development of the ego in its move toward closure and fortification. The self erects itself, solidifying and hardening in reaction to the alarming liquid-

---

[7] In order to effectively grasp the psychological dimensions of this myth, it will be useful to note the function of water in *Faust* II.iv.11106ff, and in Freud's idea of the ego as fortress. Faust, we recall, carries forth a gigantic land reclamation project near the end of his life, forcing back the element which offends him in its anarchic power and rhythmic incursions into land. This Faustian *weltbesitz* reappears in Freud as nothing less than the central task of clinical psychoanalysis: "to widen its field of vision, and so extend its organization so that it can take over new portions of the id. Where id was, there shall ego be. It is reclamation work, like the draining of the Zuyder Zee." (*New Introductory Lectures on Psychoanalysis* 106) See also Giegerich 70.

ity of the surrounding world; the ego then styles itself its own *archē*, an original and originating substance and enduring arbiter and manipulator of reality. As a crystallization of consciousness around a fixed and solid sense of self – self in opposition to form-threatening sea – the myth of the emerging ego in the Cyclopean mountain dwelling in turn parallels the pattern of primeval, elemental separation typical of cosmogonies: light and dark, sea and earth, sky and earth, cosmos and chaos. If we imagine for a moment that the Cyclops type originates in Plato's myth, then we will note that the initial vehemence of separation produces a fixed type. For the Cyclops does not evolve, despite the fact that Plato imagines tribes of these herdsmen gathering to form communities and eventually descending to build their cities in the plains after the fearful waters subside. Instead, throughout his subsequent appearances in literary history, he will remain fixed in this gesture of opposition, long after the primeval terror of the sea has faded from consciousness.

Through successive metamorphoses, Polyphemus will remain solitary, primitive, defensive and uncomprehending, a pastoral outcast doomed to re-enact again and again the role of a fossilized ego whose fixation on boundaries and possessions serves to alienate him from the pastoral commonwealth. His defensive posture, adopted out of necessity, becomes his prison, from which he hurls fatal boulders or conceives impossible loves and a wildly inflated self-image. The emphatic sense of proprietorship that we find in Theocritus and Ovid, grotesquely exaggerated by Góngora, is an important element of the egoistic mode he represents. Rosenmeyer makes the point that the Theocritean Cyclops's insistence upon an enclosed, proprietary space – a *locus inclusus* – is a specific violation of the traditionally open space of the pleasance. (202)

On the crudest level the mania for possession is simply consumption or ingestion, and the cave-dwelling can easily be seen as an extension of the stomach. Exploiting this association, Góngora designates the boulder which blocks the entrance to the cave a "mordaza," a gag: ". . . Allí una alta roca / mordaza es a una gruta de su boca." (31-32) Euripides's satyr-play *The Cyclops* takes this obsession with consumption as the center of its burlesque. Here the impious Cyclops tells Odysseus that the only sacrifices he performs are to his stomach, the greatest of deities, "god of the cave." (l. 347) His grotesque appetite, together with his stature, are what characterize him as an ogre, a voracious carnivore who happily devours lions, men, or even his own cattle.

What Ovid inherits, then, is a kind of doomed savage, a human relic whose buffoonish presence in pastoral poetry is initiated as a kind of joke: the lovesick shepherd whose melancholy yearning, like his physique, is embarrassingly disproportionate to its setting. Yet even while he is, in a sense, demoted from his former epic status as ogre to a lovesick rustic, his representation in pastoral poetry brings him nearer to a universal human type. He acquires a fantasy life, complexes and neuroses: the cave of epic becomes the psychic interior of a yearning adolescent. Theocritus portrays him, in *Idyl* XI, as a foolish bumpkin who, as Anna Rist observes, "appears unable to distinguish between the real Galatea and her appearances in dreams (ll. 22-44), and at the same time intensely – we must suppose unselfconsciously – poetic, truly the archetypal figure for the bucolic Idyll's comment on the human condition." (102) Rist calls attention to one easily overlooked factor in Cyclopean psychology, which is nonetheless present in the configuration sea-earth / nymph-giant: the Cyclops's sea-nymph mother Thoösa. As he launches into his complaint to the disdainful Galatea, Polyphemus recalls their first meeting, brought about by his mother:

> I fell in love with you maiden, the first time you came, with
> My mother,
>
> Eager to cull the bluebells from our hillside: I was your guide.
>   (26-29)

He later blames his mother for his distress, for she failed to carry his message of love to Galatea. (63-64)

The plaintive note in Polyphemus's lament is colored by his yearning for an element which is alien to him but home to his mother and his desired nymph. In his re-shaping of the tale Góngora brings this un-pastoral element, the foamy Sicilian sea, to the foreground, and in fact the interplay of earth and sea, fluidity and solidity, is a prominent feature of both his long poems. Rist sees the psychological dilemma of the Cyclops as one of transference from the mother to the nymph, involving a longing for the element of water from which he is exiled. In line 52 he regrets not having been born with gills. Theocritus's Polyphemus is, like the Platonic Cyclops, the separated one, making the best of a situation in which a natural and graceful mobility has been lost, and for which loss material prosperity and an abundance of earthly lovers is not quite adequate compensation. He must rely, finally, on "dry land" for his identity: "I too am clearly somebody, / and noticed – on dry land." (77)

Theocritus's poem addresses the problem of the "literally earthbound mortal whose eros is directed toward a being of superior order in nature." (Rist 103) Polyphemus is aware, and continues to be aware in subsequent poems, of his inferiority, for which he attempts to compensate by his boasts concerning his stature and property. Like the night sky with its multiple lights, the sea is an expanse of blueness which shelters the multiple lights of divinity, before which mortals feel acutely their fate, their limited nature as earthbound and earth-destined beings. Alberti writes, in "A la pintura," of a rain of light which is suddenly a nymph in flight which the eye wants to seize as it seizes space itself:

> Llueve la luz, y sin aviso
> ya es una ninfa fugitiva
> que el ojo busca clavar viva
> sobre el espacio mas preciso

Despite the slippage of Cyclopean song into melancholy in Theocritus's poem – "my head and both my feet are throbbing" (66) – it retreats from excessive feeling and self-pity and turns upward, leveling out into a kind of complacent acceptance of things near at hand. These are the simple tasks of everyday life, such as the tending of lambs and a lighthearted erotic satisfaction with girls of his own class. Polyphemus quickly turns away from his morbid suffering, taking himself in hand with "Cyclops, Cyclops! Where is this mad flight taking you? You'd surely show more sense if you'd keep to your basket weaving." Here there is as yet no rival, no volcanic eruption of violence, no cosmic collusion in love and death and metamorphosis. Theocritus deliberately skirts the tragic and the heroic, and the imponderable dimensions of myth, deflating the Homeric ogre to a misfit who nonetheless possesses himself sufficiently to be able to suppress the "mad flight" of Eros.

Ovid will in turn elaborate this pastoral joke by making his Polyphemus clumsier, wealthier, more boastful and more imaginative in his vain self-appraisal. Moreover, he re-incorporates the ancient folkloric and epic material in order to throw greater emphasis on the violent and grotesque side of the creature. The "Song of Polyphemus," 112 lines set within Galatea's narrative, comprises the following topics:

1) Praise of Galatea: comparisons of her beauty to shells, kids, apples, trees, grapes, etc.
2) Reproaches for hardness and obstinacy
3) Boasts of possessions: caves, apples, grapes, flocks
4) Entreaties: "lift up your shining head from the blue water"
5) Self-praise: stature, hairiness, the single bright eye
6) Complaints and threats: here thoughts of his rejection in favor of the more comely Acis prompt the jealous fantasy of his rival's dismemberment: "I will tear his guts out, I will pull him to pieces, / Scatter him over the fields and over the seas..."

In Góngora's version the giant's awareness of a rival is sudden: he sees his goats trampling on his precious grape vines and the stones he hurls at them penetrate the lovers' bower; only as he sees them flee does his rage at Acis break forth; his voice bellows like thunder and he hurls the fatal stone. After reporting her suitor's song and his murder of her lover, Ovid's Galatea closes her tale with the transformation of Acis:

> A reed grew tall, and the rock's hollow sounded
> With gushing water, and, wonderful to tell
> A youth was standing there, waist deep in the current,
> Rushes around his new-formed horns, my Acis,
> But larger than life, and with the color
> Of blue-green water gods, but still my Acis,
> Whose waters keep their former name.
>
> (891-97)

The changed Acis is still recognizable, but has become a water god, not scattered, as his murderer had intended, but whole, subsumed into a blue and fluid "artifice of eternity."

At this point it will be useful, before returning to a closer look at Góngora's poem, to sum up a number of Cyclopean themes derived from classical sources and essential to the stock Mediterranean type which will appear in renaissance poetry:

1. *The melancholy lover:* the giant shepherd's exclusion from the bower by virtue of his unseemly behavior and appearance, which carries over the pattern of his isolation in the Homeric world into the pastoral mode, and transposes the distress and insecurity caused by his blinding to amorous melancholy.
2. *The solitary dwelling:* The cave that looks out towards the sea and Galatea, and which is a symbolic extension of his appetite and desire.
3. *The catalogue of gifts:* explicit pride in wealth and pleasure in material abundance. This becomes the "cornucopia" theme in Góngora's poem.
4. *Self-regard:* The shepherd's vain self-description with its emphasis on stature, virile hairiness, and the all-seeing eye.
5. *Jealousy and violence:* The murder of Acis, precipitating the tale's crowning metamorphosis – Ovid's innovation and a favored theme in the baroque.

CHAPTER II

THE CAVERN AND THE SOLAR EYE

> "Everything Saturnine points down into the depths of the earth."
>
> Walter Benjamin

> "We *are* Time, but we *possess* also an image of history and in this image death, and with death birth, appear as the two riddles. For all other beings life pursues its course without suspecting its limits, i.e., without conscious knowledge of task, meaning, duration and object."
>
> Oswald Spengler

1. THE "CAVERNA PROFUNDA"

Solitude, writes Schopenhauer, makes the most beguiling landscape desolate and hostile for those who cannot rise above will and desire. (WWR l. 198) We see this idea of solitude in *Paradise Lost*, in which Satan is cast down into a fiery and lightless world, whose pyramidal form is the shape of the rebellious will. Satan himself takes on this shape when he "springs upward" towards earth and Eden "like a Pyramid of fire." (II.1013) The multiple light of the peacock's plumage, and the refracted light of the rainbow suspended in the air above the cataract in *Faust* II, are images of a presence beyond the reach of Faustian or Cyclopean will or desire, and yet mysteriously linked to these forces. For Schopenhauer, the contemplation of varied form, color and light is that mode of apprehension by which we are released from bondage to will and desire:

> The wholly immediate, unreflective, yet also inexpressible pleasure that is excited in us by the impression of colours,

which is strengthened by metallic lustre, and still more by transparency, as for example in stained glass windows, and even more by means of clouds and their reflection at sunset – this pleasure, I say, rests on the fact that in the easiest manner, in a manner that is almost physically necessary, the whole of our interest is here won for knowledge without any excitement of our will. (375)

The opening stanzas of the *Polifemo* figure an emphatic negation of this mode of self-transcendence. For with the depiction of the Cyclopean locale we are immediately drawn into a landscape suggestive of depth and subjectivity – the gravity and opaque solitude of self in withdrawal from light and visibility. The Cyclops and his sealed cave provide an image of the centripetal and compacted self which may or may not be dissolved in aesthetic contemplation. The Cyclopean self is an abyss expressive of both density and hollowness, and the seemingly contradictory relation of these two qualities conforms, not coincidentally, to traditional fantasies of the earth's interior. The *hollowness* of Cyclopean space is the shape of deprivation and desire, but is also the setting, as we will see in Chapter IV, for the solitary, underground forge of language.

Góngora's Sicily is a Mediterranean paradise disfigured by a rude chasm akin to Hades in its depth and sombre darkness, and in its power to violently disrupt. The cave is located in Lilybaeum, the western promontory of the island, where the poet relocates Mt. Aetna, which contains Vulcan's forge at its base. The same mass of sea-washed earth and rock alternately serves as the giant Typhon's crypt:[1]

> Donde espumoso el mar siciliano
> el pie argenta de plata al Lilibeo
> (bóveda o de las fraguas de Vulcano
> o tumba de los huesos de Tifeo)
> pálidas señas cenizoso un llano

---

[1] Don Quixote explains to the barber that giants, like other phenomena of legend, once had a literal existence: this fact is supported not only by Scripture, but by archaeological discoveries in Sicily, where "there have been found legbones and armbones so large that their size makes it plain that their owners were giants and as tall as great towers. Geometry puts this fact beyond a doubt." (II.432)

> —cuando no del sacrílego deseo—
> del duro oficio da. Allí una alta roca
> mordaza es a una gruta, de su boca.
>
>   (25-32)

> [Where, as it treads on the Sicilian surge,
> Marsala's foot is shod with silver foam
> (Either a vault that houses Vulcan's forge,
> Or serves the bones of Typhon for a tomb)
> Upon an ashy plain pale signs emerge
> From this one's sacrilegious wish, or from
> The other's toil, and there a lofty rock
> Muzzles a cave, whose mouth it seems to block.]

The poem's first stanza after the Dedication introduces the underworld of the poem, and links it to: 1. imprisonment by burial in the earth, as a punishment for rash impiety, and 2. the "duro oficio" or harsh labor of Vulcan and the "brotherhood of Aetna" who serve him in his forge. Both these figures are "cast down" – Typhon by Zeus, and Vulcan (Hephaestus) by his mother Hera, who hurls her infant son down into Hades shortly after his disappointing birth. Moreover, each becomes a source of underground fire: the one provides the controlled fire of the artisan; the other the randomly erupting fire of volcanoes. Góngora typically presents us with a complex superimposition of images. The double association is not, however, merely a gratuitous display of classical learning but a symbolic figuration of the double nature of the Cyclopean *caverna:* for the cave serves as a kind of psychic prison for a type of archaic monster allied to the underworld, akin to Typhon in his lack of regard for the Olympian gods. But it is also a place of work for a deformed and loveless artisan – a forge for Cyclopean song.

Stanza 5 (33-40) deepens the perspective of the site to suggest an even more archaic cavern which is close to original Night, child of Void or Chaos in the *Theogony:*

> Guarnición tosca de este escollo duro
> troncos robustos son, a cuya greña
> menos luz debe, menos aire puro
> la caverna profunda, que a la peña;
> caliginoso lecho, el seno obscuro

ser de la negra noche nos lo enseña
infame turba de nocturnas aves,
gimiendo tristes y volando graves.

[For garniture some rugged tree-trunks grow
Round this hard boulder, to whose matted hair
Even less the cave's recesses seem to owe
Than to the rock for light and purer air;
Above the murky den, as if to show
What black and midnight depths are hidden there,
A flock of nightly birds defiles the skies
With ponderous wings and melancholy cries.]

The "caverna profunda" of line 36 is a dark and airless place of repose – the bed of night – whose identification with "la negra noche" is reinforced by the sad and heavy flight of circling nocturnal birds. The Hesiodic prototype of this void is the abyss at the beginning of the world which is the ground from which everything begins. (II.116)

The cavern acquires a soul, an expressive interiority, in Stanza 6, in which four metaphors extend the description of the Cyclopean habitat: "melancólico vacío" is the primary equation, qualified by "bárbara choza," "albergue umbrío," and "redil espacioso."

De este, pues, formidable de la tierra
bostezo, el melancólico vacío
a Polifemo, horror de aquella sierra,
bárbara choza es, albergue umbrío,
y redil espacioso donde encierra
cuanto las cumbres ásperas, cabrío,
de los montes esconde: copia bella
que un silbo junta y un peñasco sella.

[Earth, yawning hugely, leaves a dismal space
Which makes the terror of the countryside,
The Cyclops, a barbaric dwelling-place,
A sombre shelter and a pinfold wide
In which as many of the caprine race
He may enclose as with their numbers hide
The rugged mountains, and whose comely flocks
A whistle gathers and a boulder locks.]

The poet has guided the reader from the openness and impersonality of the foamy Sicilian sea to a primeval void, and then to the morose habitation of a quasi-human being. Within this negative space, whose melancholy vacuity was introduced by the sad cries of nocturnal birds in the preceding stanza, the giant not only dwells but guards his precious goats. The space of the cave opens out to accomodate them with the fourth metaphor, "redil espacioso," but seems simultaneously to release and enclose its contents: we see them spread out over the mountainside, and then gathered into the sealed cave: expansion followed by the inevitable contraction to the immutable boundaries of the disfigured soul.

As we are concerned in this chapter with the poetic symbols for a kind of psychic imprisonment, it will be helpful to briefly review some aspects of the archetypal prison of the gods, Tartaros (from which the Middle Latin *tartarus,* or irritable, violent, intractable person). In *The Iliad* Homer places Tartaros beneath Hades, so that it forms the fourth and deepest region of the cosmos. Zeus threatens to punish any god who intervenes between the Trojans and the Greeks by casting him or her into Tartaros, "far below, where the uttermost depth of that pit lies under / earth, where there are gates of iron and a brazen doorstone, / as far beneath the house of Hades as from earth the sky lies." (8.13-16) Hesiod imagines Tartaros as a place of absolute darkness and cold originating as a "hold underneath the highways of earth." (118-119) It is so far beneath the earth that a "bronze anvil falling from the sky would fall nine days and nights and reach Tartaros on the tenth." (73) Tartaros therefore appears to have been conceived as a more negative space than original void itself, which, like earth, was an original elemental power.

In *The Aeneid* Tartaros is no deeper a region than Elysium: the path which carries Aeneas through the underworld forks after he glimpses the foggy plain where military heroes dwell: the right fork leads beneath the walls of Dis to Elysium, the left to Tartaros. The Sibyl instructs him to follow the left road. He sees a cliff at the base of which are "broad battlements triple-walled, heavily guarded and encircled by a flaming river." (549) Beyond a huge gate lies the prison ruled by Rhadamanthus, a pit of darkness which reaches down "twice as far as the eye looks up toward heaven and Olympus." (577-79) Here the tormented inhabitants, Titans and barbarous Thessalonians, serve their eternal sentences. Here are found the infernal repetitions of such punishments as Ixion's wheel, Sisiphus's rock, and the repeatedly fouled feast of the Lapiths.

Hesiod's cosmic dungeon has been subject to conflicting interpretations. Despite its evident separation in these texts from the original generative powers of earth and void, M. L. West claims that both Chaos and Tartaros should be considered not separate from earth, "but deep inside it and part of it." (118-119) James Hillman, writing from the perspective of depth psychology, insists on the essential ontological separateness of the entire underworld from nature and earth, and from our own understanding of organic life. The word "subterranean," derived from the Greek *hypogeios*, or "below Ge," "referred to the whole celestial hemisphere carved below our earth and which, like Hades, must necessarily be invisible from our perspective." (*The Dream and the Underworld* 39) What occurs in Tartaros has nothing to do, according to Hillman, with earthly matters, with *physis* – the region is absolutely severed from all that is born, fluorishes in the light and dies. Vincent Vycinas, explicating Heidegger's notion of earth and *physis*, opts for the placement of *all* subterranean powers as a kind of perennial base, withdrawn and concealed, of the Greek world and its Olympian substructure. Although mastered by Zeus, this place of origin – chaos, earth, night, etc., – is never really absent, and continues to pose a threat to the upper world. (201-02)

Returning to the metaphysics of the *Theogony*, it is not unreasonable to conceive of Tartaros as an Olympian invention in which the gods of light bury and contain the resurgent power of darkness, and by which "void" – the boundlessness and mystery of origin – is converted into a "place," heavily guarded and encircled by three walls. The "upper" underworld is reserved as a source of threat to the world of beings who thrive in the light: the volcanic crypt of Typhon or Enceladus may erupt ar random, and Hades once emerged into daylight to survey the effects of ash and flame on the Sicilian countryside, and was struck by Cupid's arrow. (*Met.* V) His enthrallment with Persephone would bring about Demeter's grief and wrath, and the brutal novelty of winter.

In pastoral reincarnations Cyclopean imprisonment becomes a cavernous prison of melancholy where a brooding subject is gathered to himself in a forlorn self-sufficiency. The Cyclops will therefore evoke not only the spherical shape implicit in his name, but also the pressure of containment and circumscription suggested by the lineage of his cave. He will strive to identify himself with a solar, patriarchal deity while remaining rooted to the source of his malady, the *caverna profunda*. The monstrous singularity of Odysseus's adversary is reinforced by the frustration of his monstrous desire, and the cavern deepens into boundlessness.

While it reverberates with the memory of the cosmic prison which are its antecedents, the *caverna* is also a place of ingestion, and Góngora's Cyclops is distinguished in part by the attention given to the colossal scale of his consumerism, as well as by a preoccupation with containing or hiding the goods in which he shows such pride. The oral symbolism of Stanza 4, "Allí una alta roca / mordaza es a una gruta de su boca," suggests the voraciousness which has generally been an attribute of ogres in mythology and folklore. The cave itself, in Stanza 6, functions as an enclosure for the giant's herd of goats ("redil espacioso,") (45) and a series of images associated with the Cyclops and his passion for possession suggest concavity, concealment, enclosure or engorgement. The beehives are hidden in the tree, and the giant's wallet *(zurrón)* is stuffed to bursting with a harvest of fruits and nuts. (Stanzas 10,11) The giant's goats are so numerous that they hide the mountain; a tall tree provides a site for the delectable alchemy of honey production and storage, and concealment from the greedy goats (St. 50); and even the fatal rock which Polyphemus hurls at Acis, compared to an urn and a pyramid, figures an attempt to confine and suppress, fatal missile and tomb collapsed into a single image.

As Cyclopean appetite and subjectivity, the "caverna profunda" is a type of counter-cosmos, a black hole which draws towards its dark and confined space the contents of an entire world. The cavern as a principle of telluric concealment, of things buried in the earth, hidden from light, is in direct conflict with the law of *physis*, which is a coming forth into the light, a "rising or breaking through, unravelling, opening, developing." (Vycinas 136) The Cyclops as telluric monster is the depth of earth which hides from light. And as a human monster he manifests his resistance to *physis* in his scorn of custom *(nomos)* and morals *(ethos)*, a trait to which Homer gives particular attention. For *physis* governs not only biological processes but the social structures which contain and "bring forward" human life.[2]

In addition to shading the characterization of Polyphemus in the direction of the abysmal, the *gestalt* of concealment plays another role equally innovative, and typical of Góngora's descriptive technique. To disguise or conceal implies, in this context, a hidden motive in nature itself, a somewhat disquieting subjectivity which qualifies the pristine appearance of natural beings. The world the poem presents is one known in an undulation of display, whose beings simultaneously turn towards and away from their spectators, flaunting their duplicity. These apparitions, often qualified, even hesitant, are not quite "del candor primero," not precisely candid. Sicily both conceals and reveals its wealth; the harvested apple disguises its inner candor; the gold of honey is hidden in the trunks of trees and selectively displayed. Things are displayed in the light, in the "clearing" of the poem, but they retain a hiddenness, an affinity for the opacity of earth, and for their own non-being. Logically enough, light itself is frequently uncertain in both Góngora's long poems; the poise of twilight and the alternation of light and dark are usually more compelling to the poet than full noon – the hour of the rapt philosopher.[3]

2. The "melancólico vacío": Time, Subjectivity and Melancholy

The depth and interiority of the cave, as the sixth stanza indicates, are not merely spatial phenomena but constitute the shape of the Cyclops' solitude. As a site of introspection, solitude and desire, the cave is the nothingness experienced by the suffering

---

[2] *Physis*, notes Heidegger, was not restricted by the early Greeks to physical life but meant "that which arises." See *Poetry Language Thought* 100.

[3] It is both the hour of fullest consciousness and maximum lucidity, and the hour of rapt unconsciousness in the "noon" passage (275-278) in Nietzsche's *Thus Spoke Zarathustra*. A golden plenitude is evoked, and also a longing to be engulfed by the "cheerful, dreadful abyss of noon," in diction which curiously echoes Andrew Marvell's "On a Drop of Dew." The theme in Nietzsche is highly enigmatic. Noon stands for the moment of supreme affirmation, and yet Nietzsche's favourite painter is Claude Lorrain, autumnal painter of twilit harbors. Twilight is to high noon, perhaps, what Ariadne is to Zarathustra; yet Nietzsche is the first to admit that this is a riddle. Perhaps a *musical* riddle.

self, the cavernous depths of self deprived of the boundaries of aesthetic delight. The withdrawal from space into the void of the cave is withdrawal into that internal state which Kant correlates with the time-dimension: as space is the dimension of the phenomena of external sense, time is an internal form of perception linked to the intuition of self and one's internal state. (26,30) Like an island, the cavern circumscribes, isolating its inhabitant, dooming him to an existence from which the other two figures of the fable, the lovers, enjoy a dispensation. For they belong to that class of beings for whom "life pursues its course without suspecting its limits," (Spengler 166) existing chiefly within the speechless world of their blissful mutual regard, an idyllic area of enthrallment. Like flowers or fish, these inhuman lovers have their being by virtue of a particular structure, while the monster exists in the instability of his desire, which burgeons on the stimulus of his memory. Desire and memory constitute the temporal boundaries of his interior world.

The frustration of Cyclopean desire converts melancholy longing to jealous rage; this rage in turn becomes a scythe, forecast in l. 356 as "segur de los celos," which cuts down his rival and brings the fable to its close. The scythe of jealousy is also the scythe of time which severs the present moment from consciousness, defeating the suspended moment of pastoral.[4] The Stoics merged the identity of the arch-ogre Kronos, who devoured his own children after being warned that one of them would overthrow him, with that of Chronos – Time. For, as they observed, not only did Time devour, but it was thought to be bound by the course of the stars just as Kronos was bound and imprisoned by Zeus. (Klibansky 139) History, as Stephen Daedalus knew, is Cyclopean, and the Cyclops functions in this poem as an agent of time, and of Saturnine time-consciousness. His song stretches backwards and forwards, disturbing the *nunc stans* of antique sea and pastoral meadow with an insistency of memory and stridency of longing: He remembers an earlier, more savage self, which gives way to the

---

[4] Marvell's Mower, a variant of the Renaissance Polyphemus, sees his own reflection in his scythe, "As in a crescent Moon the sun" ("Damon the Mower," l. 60), and, distracted by his sorrows, swings the blade around into his own ankle, "and there among the Grass fell down, / By his own Scythe, the Mower mown." (79-80)

role of civil host of wanderers and shipwrecked sailors; and he anticipates possession, the beatitude of fulfillment which would occur if only Galatea would respond to his imperatives, "Deja las ondas," "pisa la arena," "escucha un día / mi voz . . ." Abandon the waves, step down on sand, listen one day to my voice.

The Cyclops, then, is the only one of the three figures to address himself to the full range of temporality. But Cyclopean time is above all a time of expectancy, the dimension prepared for the advent of Galatea, of the goddess – a time aspiring to radiant spaciousness. What is missing is the present moment, the ecstatic "now" which her appearance would bestow.

Singing, Polyphemus seeks reprieve from the sound of his own voice even while he glories in it. He anticipates the light that will silence the terrible sound of his yearning, its *reverberation*. The Cyclops *is* a penetrating sound; he is megaphonic, a monstrous acoustics; and it is not difficult to recognize the resemblance of his cave to a sounding chamber, or even to the organ of hearing itself, the physical sense which has an invisible, internal dimension with its passageway (auditory canal) and its vibrating inner chamber. Acis and Galatea are notably silent, absorbed in one another's gaze, and the contrast between their silence and the horrendous sound of Polyphemus's pipes is as striking as the contrast between the light and darkness that symbolizes the presence of monster and nymph. Acis watches the sleeping nymph while drinking from the spring beside her:

> su boca dio, y sus ojos cuanto pudo,
> al sonoro cristal, al cristal mudo.
>
> (191-2)
>
> [The sounding crystal to his lips he raises,
> And sidelong on the silent crystal gazes.]

He then places pastoral tributes at her side, and lies down in the grass, feigning sleep. Galatea, discovering the gifts, glimpses the figure of Acis in her imagination before she discovers him "sleeping" in the grass:

> ni lo ha visto, si bien el pincel süave
> lo ha bosquejado en su fantasía.
>
> (251-52)

The paintbrush, *pincel*, is the arrow of Cupid which colors her imagination while it pierces her heart.

The two lovers are idols to one another, and their courtship consists entirely of silent mutual admiration. The description of their encounter features words denoting watchfulness, appearance, semblance, admiration and display. Only with the Cyclopean destruction of the bower are these two set in motion, the one "fugitiva nieve," (482) the other "corriente plata" (501), and even here their flight is silent, except in the penultimate stanza when Galatea is reported to call on the sea gods to save the form of her shattered lover.

A parallelism between the intense seeing that occurs in the bower and the monstrous sound of the shepherd's pipes is developed in images of multiplied sight and amplified sound. By the invisible power of his voice Polyphemus ritualistically calls forth an unseen power – or tries to. But in the stanza preceding his song (12), the poet inserts the idea of sound multiplied one-hundredfold – the sound of the giant's bagpipes is magnified by "cien cañas," one hundred reeds, and the resulting "barbarous sound" is in turn multiplied in even more echoes than there are reeds:

> cera y cáñamo unió (que no debiera)
> cien cañas, cuyo bárbaro ruido,
> de mas ecos que unió cáñamo y cera
> albogues, duramente es repetido.
> La selva se confunde, el mar se altera,
> rompe Tritón su caracol torcido,
> sordo huye el bajel a vela y remo:
> tal la música es de Polifemo!

> [A hundred pipes with wax and string are joined
> (A horrid din the vile contrivance makes);
> As many echoes as the pipes combined
> By string and wax the raucous music wakes.
> The tree-tops toss, the surges crash and grind,
> His trump of twisted nacre Triton breaks,
> Fear wings with sail or oar the deafened boats:
> So barbarous are Polyphemus' notes!]

When the Cyclops fills the pipes with breath from the "prodigioso fuelle," or bellows of his mouth, Cyclopean song imposes its monstrous depths, the depths of the cavern, on the landscape, resounding in more than one hundred echoes.[5] The repeated sound forces a rupture in sea and woods. Nature recoils from this aggressive dissonance, and the marine gods flee.

The lovers' courtship is initiated by a "rhetorical silence" – the cunning strategy of Acis whose seduction of Galatea is carried out by means of a careful, watchful passivity. In Stanza 37 he watches the nymph like "Argos," that is, with a hundred eyes, while she in turn watches his apparently sleeping figure:

> Acis –aún más de aquello que dispensa
> la brújula del sueño vigilante–,
> alterada la ninfa esté o suspensa,
> Argos es siempre atento a su semblante,
> lince penetrador de lo que piensa,
> cíñalo bronce o múrelo diamante:
> que en sus paladiones Amor ciego,
> sin romper muros, introduce fuego.
>
> [Acis, more watchful than the tiny space
> His eyelids, feigning sleep, might seem to grant,
> Intent as Argus, scans the maiden's face,
> Now agitated and now hesitant.
> Lynx-like he strives her inmost thoughts to trace
> Though girt with bronze and walled with adamant:
> Blind Love, although he breaks no ramparts down,
> Leads in the Trojan horse and fires the town.]

Sight, like sound, is shown to be active to the point of having a projectory force, and it is also multiplied one-hundredfold, but in a context of mutual attraction, of erotic correspondence and reciprocity. Here is an example of how the poem's allusiveness works towards a carefully orchestrated unfolding of an image in the mind. For the comparison of Acis to Argus "unfolds" the notion

---

[5] The echo is a popular device of baroque music, especially in Monteverdi. Thomas Mann interprets its use thus: "The echo, the giving back of the human voice as nature-sound, and the revelation of it as nature-sound, is essentially a lament: nature's melancholy 'Alas!' in view of man, her effort to utter his solitary state." (Dr. *Faustus* 486)

of intense vision into the one hundred eyes of Argus; this unfolding image in turn links up with an entire pattern of vision in the poem, but also reminds us of the one hundred-reed pipe of the giant, so that the poet has delicately balanced two movements "hacia afuera": the movement outwards of the barbarous music, which imposes the depth of Cyclopean perspective onto the classical pastoral world of the lovers, and the intensification of vision, which opens up, "lightens," rather than penetrates the world.[6]

The inhuman lovers seem to exist like silent images on a screen, in a magic precinct which may be transformed but not destroyed, and their silence seems to be a feature of their dispensation from the specific intoxications of utterance, and from mortality.[7] While they retire to their bower, Polyphemus prepares his song. The time of the song is the specific modality of human existence and of human suffering and desire. The Cyclops' suffering is projected outwards, forcing change, death, a permanent alteration in the environment; time is *implanted* in the landscape, and the tableau of Acis and Galatea, a cosmos unknown to Cyclopean (or Faustian) consciousness, becomes a history – a fable.

Calderón's *Auto del divino Orfeo*, an allegory of the Fall and Redemption, includes a vivid and compelling stage image of time as a kinetic *chiaroscuro* of being and non-being. Human time as expectation is illustrated by the anguished consequences of Eve / Eurydice's act of disobedience. The dark-cloaked figure of Envy, the double of the Prince of Shadows, interposes himself between

---

[6] For the hundred eyes of Argus, see Ovid, *Met* I: Juno, ever suspicious of her husband, places Io, turned into a heifer by Jove, under surveillance by her watchdog Argus. "Argus the star-eyed" is able to keep watch even in his sleep, for as he closes two eyes, the others remain fixed in Io. Jove, pitying Io's suffering, sends Mercury to kill the monster. This he accomplishes by lulling Argus to sleep with a reed pipe, and then severing his head: "... So Argos / lay low, and all the light in all those eyes / Went out forever, a hundred eyes, one darkness. / And Juno took the eyes and fastened them on the feathers of a bird of hers, the peacock, / So that the peacock's tail is spread with jewels." (719-24)

[7] Robert Jammes, who views the poem in terms of a love story, describes the episode (St. 23-42) of Acis and Galatea as "the birth of love in the heart of a virgin," citing these middle stanzas as evidence that Góngora was a more sentimental poet than critics have wanted to believe. (541) But the eroticism of these verses seems barely touched by sentiment, and it is hard to discern the "heart palpitations" that Jammes claims for them. In fact what is represented is the intense mutual attraction of idealized and approximate *images* of human beings – hardly human at all.

the dancers who represent the primal, luminous Days – "el candor primero." By joining their serene procession he stealthily instigates a rhythm; each successive re-positioning of darkness between the sedate *pasando* of the days imposes a renewed *anticipation* of light, a mirage of possibilities within which a destiny, or even a reprieve, might be improvised. (*Obras completas* III)

Polyphemus takes this role in the poem, but as a human rather than a supernatural force. He is the instigator, the spoiler, the prospector and generator of illusion, disillusion, loss, rumor and clamor. He creates event out of nothingness, void, absence. Desire draws him from his cave, and his appearance on earth will wrench earth into a world whose gods are terrorized into withdrawal – withdrawal from the inexorable drive towards debasement and disfigurement which will mark the progress of the human will.

Polyphemus, then, introduces into the *locus amoenus* the malaise of history and desire. Moreover, with each reference to Polyphemus we are further involved in a web of allusion which generates a depth of perspective behind the figure of the giant. As we read, a host of associations accumulates: we are led to think of the rebellious Typhon, and the defeat and imprisonment of various figures representing chthonic power; then, the cuckolded and lame artisan Vulcan and his improbable marriage to Venus; the cannibalistic Cyclops of Homer and folklore, the plaintive lovers of pastoral tradition, and even Satan looking on with envy at the Edenic couple. This network of allusions heightens the incongruity of the Cyclops' presence in the pastoral community. Another, implicit component in this complex of literary and mythological associations is Saturn, and in fact the Janus-faced nature of the Cyclops, as monster and poet, pastoral goatherd and figure of the underworld, is a product of the same imaginative impulse which engendered he complexity of the myth of the Roman agricultural god. With the Roman conflation of Kronos and Saturn, traits thought to derive from the planetary influence of Saturn – greed, bitterness, autocratic behavior – were combined with the earlier negative features of the Greek god (celibacy, captivity, violence) to produce the saturnine type, or *humor melancholicus*.[8] The developing

---

[8] Material concerning the theory of melancholy in the ancient world is taken from Klibansky *et. al., Saturn and Melancholy.*

astrological thought of late antiquity designates the planet Saturn as the ruler of the destiny of the melancholic, who is held to be cold, pessimistic, greedy and tenacious.

Despite these originally negative attributes, Saturn eventually acquires an aura of privileged destiny, becoming, in the Italian Renaissance, symbolic of a type of transcendental awareness.[9] The evolution of Saturn towards his exalted state in Renaissance Neo-Platonic thought seems to repeat the pattern of the earlier ambivalence of Kronos who, although the castrator of his own children, was nonetheless believed to have presided over the Golden Age. In Ficino's thought the Saturnine type is a solitary misfit who possesses an exceptional degree of self-awareness and creative genius; hence the somewhat romantic conception of genius as monster – a man who, deficient in humanity, as commonly understood, experiences himself as a centripetal force, and for whom the surrounding space of the world serves as the medium of his self-realization, an alembic in which man-as-abyss becomes luminous and transcendent. The Cyclopean cave itself, as an oral symbol, suggests this Saturnine duality: for the mouth signifies transcendence as the organ of speech (disclosure), and destruction as the organ of ingestion (concealment).[10]

The melancholy type, then, solitary, greedy, potentially dangerous, is the human equivalent to the *caverna profunda* in its relation to pastoral, and its threat to pastoral equanimity. Like time itself, it is an enemy to otium, and to the entire floating world of

---

[9] The are repeated references to Saturn in the letters of Ficino and his Florentine friends. Ficino alternately refers to the "gifts" and to the curse of Saturn. In a letter to Giovanni Cavalcanti, to whom he had complained in an earlier letter of his Saturn-induced depression, he writes "Saturn seems to have impressed the seal of melancholy on me from the beginning..." and he goes on to comfort himself with "this nature itself is a unique and divine gift." (*Letters* 33-34)

[10] Long before the European Renaissance vogue of the Saturnine "curse" of genius the association of Saturn with melancholy was promoted in the writings of Arab scholars. Abu Masar (d. 885) writes of the nature of Saturn that it is "cold, dry, bitter, black, dark, violent and harsh" and claims that Saturn rules over husbandry and farming, the measuring and division of things, and sponsors the traits of unsociability, ostentation, boastfulness and rage. (Klibansky 130, 131) By the twelfth century the idea of the Saturnine was being revised and coordinated with the Galenic tradition of the humors. Black bile, the humor supposed to be responsible for the melancholy disposition, was thought by Hugo de Foulloi (d. 1174) to increase it presence in the body in autumn. (Klibansky 107-09)

pastoral, which is meant to seem ego-less and timeless. It is the fissure in the earth through which such *kore* as Eurydice and Persephone tumble down to Hades, and by which the soul is drawn down to its own depths. Saturn, as a planetary influence to which we are susceptible when alone and idle, according to Ficino, "devours" his own sons—those who are born under his influence—by enticing them to contemplation, "cutting them off from the earth with a kind of scythe if they are lingering too long there." (*De vita triplici.* 66) Melancholy is the scythe which severs us from the natural and social worlds, just as Chronos is the scythe that severs us from the present moment. It encourages, writes Ficino, a gathering in of the personality towards its center, away from the circumference: "to be fixed at the center is very much like being at the center of the earth itself, which resembles black bile." (5-6) Saturn is the planet of the senex, and of all "separated ones" cut off from the rest of the human race, "separated from others, either divinely or brutishly, blessed or pressed by extreme misery." (92)

3. The Underworld and Formal Deficiency

The *caverna profunda*, as we have seen, is a figure of negation on a number of levels: as an abyss or chasm, or as interiority and depth, it is a spatial negation which specifically challenges the world of surface phenomena constitutive of the pastoral locale— the pastoral meadows of the nymphs Eurydice, Persephone, and Galatea; as a place of darkness it is a negation of the light of *physis* and of those things which are made manifest and flourish in the light; as a solitary dwelling, a place where the isolated self confronts its nothingness, it negates the values of plurality and association which are fundamental to the pastoral mode. (Rosenmeyer 202) And as a place of concealment and hoarding it is inimical to disclosure, to the "rising to the surface" which characterizes what I have chosen to call the Venusian aesthetic. It is this last sense of Cyclopean negation which brings us to the question of form and of the monster as anti-form, or deformity. For monsters occupy a place between utter chaos and the forms of the upper world; they are only partially disclosed, only imperfectly and uneasily at home in the world of appearances.

The monstrous, long associated with the underworld and nature's depths, poses a threat of regression, of a return to origins, and so reminds us of time, causality and death, realities starkly at odds with the pastoral fantasy which typically seeks a mood of benign stasis. Monstrosity in the form of giants, ogres, or dragons represents a deficiency of form which Aristotle thought to be the result of the resistance of matter, and proof of the contingency which constitutes nature. Later thinkers such as Pliny and Augustine would seek in monstrous phenomena clues to human destiny and signs of an imaginative deity who enjoyed evoking wonder and admiration in his creatures. (Céard 3) The role of the monstrous in literature often suggests that it is a revelation of absurdity in the universe, and a reminder of the fragility of cosmos and the possibility of a return to original chaos and meaninglessness. Monsters are those beings which are closest to the earliest deities, archaic Void, Earth, Night (whom Milton calls "uncreated" and "unessential" [*PL* II.150,439], that is, lacking in being, monstrous) and to the Hesiodic progeny of Night – Destruction, Death, Vengeance and Strife.

Góngora's version of the Cyclops story is in fact framed by two absurdities or monstrosities which challenge the natural order of things: first, at the beginning of the poem, the dominating cavern and its inhabitant, both of which may be regarded as a disfigurement of the pastoral Sicilian landscape. Second, and forming the poem's denouement, is the absurdity of metamorphosis, in which the resistance of matter is symbolically overcome, and the violent eruption of the Cyclops canceled. It is one of Góngora's innovations, and a function of his reflexive art, to stress the image of the cave in such a way that it is placed in a polar relationship to metamorphosis, thereby enhancing the creation of new form from the shattered body of Acis. Balanced against its opposing image, the metamorphosis which transforms the blood of Acis into a river is an assertion of creative power, of the power of the imagination to transform the world. These poles, deficient form and transformation (and the magic of transformation is never far from the monstrous in mythical thinking) have in common their seizure of the surrounding world, their gathering of meaning into themselves. For the cave is a metonymy for the brooding power of its inhabitant, who claims to be an "arbiter" of reality, superior to the gods themselves; and metamorphosis asserts the perennial generative power of the world he has failed to control. While each in its way is a violation of the integrity of form, metamorphosis acts as a correction to monstrosity and the effects of its activation – Cyclopean violence and the *sparagmos* of Acis. And when we consider the power of melancholy to paralyze the artist it is, more importantly, a symbolic defeat of the melancholy figured in the cavern.

If the *caverna profunda* is a metonymic extension of Cyclopean presence, and so a symbol of fatality within the poem as garden, then at the further "end" of the poem metamorphosis supplies the means to integrate this fatality into the pastoral order by lifting the pastoral to a higher level of sublimation, symbolized by the silver-white water (in Ovid it is blue) of the river. This reading explicitly challenges those readings which view the Cyclops as the poet's means of destroying the pastoral world; for the flowing water of the poem's concluding lines is a sublimation of the victim's blood and aestheticizes the earth over which it flows. In this way it is the artist's response to the devouring void which threatens the cessation of all movement, change and creation. It is a concentrated image of the process of turning life and the destruction of life into art.

4. The Cavern and the Solar Eye

While the Cyclops' status as monster resides first in his gigantic size, his single eye, like his cave dwelling, resonates beyond the context of his physical deformity to become a symbol of a particular, and human, orientation towards the world. We encounter it first in Stanza 7, parenthetically enclosed in the metaphor which equates the Cyclops' stature with a mountain:

> Un monte era de miembros eminente
> este (que, de Neptuno hijo fiero,
> de un ojo ilustra el orbe de su frente,
> émulo casi del mayor lucero)

> [Of human limbs a lofty mountain made
> The Cyclops seemed, Poseidon's savage son,
> The broad horizon of whose brow displayed
> A single eye, the rival of the sun;]

Here the poet alludes to the giant's later equation of himself with solar divinity, "el mayor lucero," suggesting both the giant's traditional Promethean disregard for the primacy of the gods, and the supremely bright star of Lucifer.[11]

The god-rivaling eye denotes a pride which is openly avowed in Stanza 53, where Polyphemus assumes an Olympian pose on a cliff, rejoicing in the spectacle of his own reflection in the halcyon-stilled sea:

> Marítimo alcïón, roca eminente
> sobre sus huevos coronaba, el día
> que espejo de zafiro fue luciente
> la playa azul de la persona mía;
> miréme, y lucir vi un sol en mi frente,
> cuando en el cielo un ojo se veía:
> neutra el agua dudaba a cuál fe preste:
> o al cielo humano o al cíclope celeste.

> [The halcyon brooded on her nest one day,
> Crowning a rock that overhung the sea,
> While, bright and blue beneath, the ocean lay
> To make a sapphire looking-glass for me.
> I saw the shining sun my brows display,
> When in the sky a single eye was seen:
> The waters doubted if there shone on high
> A heavenly Cyclops or a human sky.]

It is a moment of pure vision, like the image of Narcissus himself, and figures, similarly, both fixation and separation, an endless longing and a failure to possess.

The overtones of deification in the eye-sun conceit of stanza 7 are reinforced in the later stanza through an implicit allusion to another tale from the *Metamorphoses*, in which Helios boasts that he is the "eye of the world" who sees all things and through which all men see everything – a kind of absolute perspective. (IV.230) Helios, stalking Leucothoe, boasts of his optical prowess, which allows him to master all of reality, and to supervise in turn the

---

[11] The comparison of the Cyclops' eye to the sun-god occurs in *The Aeneid* III.635-37, and in *Met.* XIII.851-53. In Ovid Polyphemus boasts that his monocular prowess is equivalent to that of Helios.

vision of mortals: "... I am the one who measures / The long year out, / I see all things, and all men / See everything through me, the eye of the world." (225-26) He allows no concealing shadows, no places where beings may be other than objects to his terrible gaze. The effect of his obsessive surveillance of Leucothoe is to oppressively lengthen the day, for "he would rise too early / From the Eastern sky, would sink too late to Ocean." (196-97)

If the cavern threatens concealment and invisibility, the relentless supervision of the Cyclopean solar eye connotes a merciless over-exposure. The Cyclops, like Helios, is a watcher, scanning the ocean for a glimpse of Galatea when he is not admiring his own reflection (he is also blinded by love, l. 341, and the high cliff of his surveillance is a "blind lantern" l. 344). His eye, like the cave, signifies a relational deformity, a seizure of reality which attempts to dominate "from above" (overseeing) as the cave dominates "from below" (ingestion). For here the solar Polyphemus towers above the world, experiencing himself a pure ego, absolutely separate from and dominant to the surrounding world. It is as though a mirage of omnipotence arose from the mere appetite represented by the cave.

As the poem moves into this "framing" stanza, it seems to slow, almost to freeze into a hypnotic stillness. Everything seems designed to support Cyclopean ego as a solid, enduring center of meaning, the focal point of an entire universe. Sea and sun are its props and reflectors. One irony in the portrayal of the Cyclops is that while he is represented as plaintively yearning for the possession of a superior being, and is perceived as the only mortal of the three figures, he perceives himself as possessing god-like powers. And yet his solidity is eventually rendered illusory to the reader, for his presence is eclipsed at the conclusion of his interrupted song, by the ecstatic poetics of metamorphosis. The myth of the Cyclops is the myth of the ego, of the "monstrosity of subjectivism" (Heidegger, "The Age of the World-view" 12) which is the subject as conscious object, a solid and closed thing, the self in its delusion of security from pain and death. (Zimmerman 47-49)

The "solar eye" passage represents the construction of an ideal self over an abyss, a foundation of void, just as the cosmos itself and the Pantheon of Olympus with its patriarch at the apex is founded upon the apparent defeat of Night and Void and their troublesome progeny. The myth of the ego is a myth of control and the Cyclops imagines his single eye to be the tool by which he "charts" and "frames" his surroundings. Each image, the cave and the solar eye, represents a would-be center of the world of sea and woods and meadow; each exerts an insistent pull on its environment. But while the cave habitat and the savage appearance of the Cyclops disqualify him from admittance into pastoral society, the single eye serves as an even more potent symbol of his psychic deformity and radical isolation. It is the perceptual extension of the abysmal cave, in that it figures the reduction of manifold reality to a single obsession. And it is, like the cave, a vortex into which everything may disappear.

Philosophically, the Cyclopean mode of perception is equivalent to ideology as a comprehensive set of ideas which makes an inflexible assertion about the nature of the world; politically it is comparable to autocracy, as we saw in Plato, and temperamentally it is manifested in Saturnine melancholy. In Stanza 53 it displaces the *caverna profunda* as the primary Cyclopean symbol. The *site* of monoptical perception, the cliff, is like the cavern a metonymic substitution. Both are figures of affliction – melancholy and blindness. The cave has matted hair, a mouth, depth and blackness; the cliff-watchtower is a blind sentry, in the same stanza (43) that the Cyclops is "de amor el fiero jayán ciego," a fierce giant blinded by love. There is a grammatical ambiguity in this passage which results in the confusion of the Cyclops, climbing the cliff at sunset, with the cliff itself:

> la cerviz oprimió a una roca brava,
> que a la playa, de escollos no desnuda,
> linterna es ciega y atalaya muda.
>   (342-44)

> [. . . the savage giant came
> His ponderous foot upon a cliff to lay
> Which, soaring high, surveyed the rock-strewn coast,
> An eyeless light, a silent sentry-post.]

In line 341 Polyphemus is characterized as blinded by love, "de amor el fiero jayán ciego," so that the adjective "ciego/a" is used twice in the same stanza, first to describe the state of being blinded by love ("Amor ciego" of Stanza 37.295), and then to describe the cliff as a "blind" lantern or lighthouse, a lighthouse without a light: mute, without signals. Góngora is playing off the reader's awareness of the tale of the Cyclops' blinding by Odysseus, but why a blind, mute cliff? Is the cliff the base of the lighthouse, the Cyclops its extinguished or equivocal light? The combined effect of the two intertwined images is of height, dominance over the beach below, brilliant but faulty illumination, affliction. The passage is then followed by 1) the sound of the pipes, which cancels the muteness of "atalaya muda," and 2) images of vision and light which supersede the blindness of the Cyclops/cliff/tower.

The Cyclops' eye, in Stanza 53, becomes a light, comparable to the sun itself, and the sea below, becalmed by the nesting halcyon, becomes a mirror, "espejo de zafiro," reflecting back the light to the self-enthralled giant. The sea is reduced from the generative *aphros* of the "reino de la espuma" to a flat, reflecting surface which negates its own depths and capacity for gratuitous creation. An absolute equality is established between the images of the sun and the Cyclopean eye, while the water, otherwise in the poem mobile, and a home for the gods, becomes fixed, frozen under the Cyclops' gaze, and is unable to distinguish between the images of sun and Cyclops which it reflects: "neutra el agua dudaba..."

Heidegger describes this stance towards the world as "positioning": man brings the world "into position," reframing it according to his objectives: "The Open becomes an object and is twisted around toward the human being. Over against the world as the object, man stations himself and sets himself up..." (*Poetry Language Thought* 110) The "openness" of the uncharted world occurs in Góngora's metaphysics as *aphros*, which is leveled out, relieved of its generative texture and re-positioned as a mirror, "espejo de zafiro." While we must take care to distinguish the aestheticized sea of the poet from the mirroring sea of the Cyclops (see Chapter IV), the *aplanissement* which occurs here belongs to a program of self assertion which tends to objectify the world and, according to Heidegger, to prepare it for its function as raw material.[12] This crucial act of positioning underlies the nature of technology, in relation to which man himself becomes a mere

---

[12] Marten Nøjgaard's study of Baudelaire's antipathy towards and *aplanissement* of sea depth is somewhat helpful on this point. (57-60)

functionary, underscoring his kinship with the archaic trio of weaponsmakers exploited by Zeus and Hephaestus.[13]

There are three centers of vision or reflection in this passage, each occupying its own level of the cosmos: sun, sea, and Cyclops. The middle level, that of the Cyclops, absorbs the other two, as an assertion of the primacy of human perception and of the human "positioning" of reality; the human regard usurps the regard of other beings. By his complete assimilation of the attributes of solar divinity Polyphemus styles himself "arbiter" of reality, "arbitro de montañas y riberas," as he is named in Stanza 44, l. 345. His super-vision momentarily "frames" reality, as he implicitly declares that everything can be grasped, seized, known by this magical solar perception. A reinforcement of this assertion, of the ocular power to scan and seize, occurs in Stanza 61, when, after hurling the stone at the delinquent goat, Polyphemus spies the frightened lovers fleeing their bower:

> Viendo el fiero jayán, con paso mudo
> correr al mar la fugitiva nieve
> (que a tanta vista el líbico desnudo
> registra el campo de su adarga breve
> y al garzón viendo, . . .

> [When the grim giant saw what silent haste
> Her flying snowflakes made to gain the shore
> (For his sharp glance could reach the Libyan waste
> And scan the shields its naked warriors bore),
> While Acis followed, . . .]

---

[13] Helios and the Cyclopean eye, figures of centralized and oppressive light, suggest metaphors for the concept of metaphysical truth which Heidegger deconstructs in *Being and Time* (55-58; 257f). Truth *(logos)* as judgement, an operation performed by a human subject upon an object, disregards the self-witholding of things which is integral to truth as *a-letheia*, unconcealment. Hans-Georg Gadamer explicates the "privative" concept of truth as a "taking away by force, which lifts that which is concealed out of darkness into brightness – and which has led as a final consequence to the explanatory character of European science..." Truth as *a-letheia*, in contrast, includes a residue of self-concealment, a shadow. The resistance of things to full explication is the nymph who appears and disappears, a flickering light.

Polyphemus' powers of surveillance, his power to *register* forms and events in distant space, extend as far as the coast of Africa, where even the shields of the Libyan natives do not escape his eye.

Insofar as he can sustain the illusion of omnipotence and omniscience, Polyphemus combats the sinking and diminishing inwardness of *dolor interno* (l. 466) through the colossal distortions of his ego which poses as *arbitro* of everything outside of itself. The cloud-encircled mountain cannot equal the lofty Cyclopean reach, by which Polyphemus inscribes his misfortunes on the puny dome of heaven, as less lofty suitors might inscribe their amorous messages on trees:

> Qué mucho, si de nubes se corona
> por igualarme la montaña en vano,
> y en los cielos, desde esta roca, puedo
> escribir mis desdichas con el dedo?
> (413-16)

> [No mountain, piling clouds upon it head,
> Can match my stature, for although my feet
> Are on this rock, my fingers, stretched on high,
> Can write my amorous sorrows on the sky.]

The inscription of his song and sorrows on the world articulates a myth of the self, and endows a heretofore abysmal and mute anguish with a mythology of amorous desire and suffering. He thereby gives form to himself as well as to the elusive object of his desire, partially redeeming himself from his own monstrosity.

We have moved, then, from the mute darkness of the *üntermensch* to the mountainous and brilliantly illuminated sphere of delusion belonging to the *übermensch*. It is significant that the primary fantasies of the Cyclops, of his own being and of the love-object Galatea, are expressed in images of light and vision, like candles lit against the shadows of doubt and inner pain. But his song too is deficient, for the narrator tells us, following Ovid, that the song breaks off when the giant sees his goats trampling the young shoots of his grape vines:

> Su horrenda voz, no su dolor interno
> cabras aquí le interrumpieron cuantas

> —vagas el pie, sacrílegas el cuerno—
> a Baco se atrevieron en sus plantas.
>
> (465-68)
>
> [Some goats, who dare to interrupt in scorn
> His dreadful voice, though not his inner woe,
> With heedless foot and sacrilegious horn
> Assail the plot where Bacchus' tendrils grow.]

The inspired lover reverts to the mere proprietor, and song deteriorates into a bellow of rage at the offending goats.

And the Cyclopean gaze is flawed, for he is a *human* sun, a Helios with a shadow of vulnerability. The solar eye turns in on itself; the exalted torchlight-consciousness it represents is also consciousness of deprivation. Polyphemus not only casts an immense shadow; he *is* a shadow: he shadows the world and he shadows himself as well, grasping at more light, which he is finally unable to quantify. And his vulnerability is also indicated by the very posture that asserts his power. While positioning himself to optical advantage, he also positions himself to be seen. He names himself, shows himself, brings himself forth from cavernous anonymity, and while his inwardness is superseded by a claim on the word, the claim itself exposes him to the gaze of the world. Like the sun-kings of the baroque era, he is ideally empowered and ideally contained, the supreme object as well as subject.[14] The

---

[14] The cliff is a *vantage* point, a point of advantage for an ideal viewer, and as such reflects the royalist perspective of the baroque era. Two examples demonstrate how space was engineered in order to ensure an ideal, centralized optical point of observation for a monarch. The first is the king's pavillion in the menagerie at Versailles. The Royal zoo was designed by Le Vaux so that the king could observe his animals from an octagonal glass pavillion that looked out onto the cages. (Foucault 203) The second example, from the Stuart court, is more pertinent and more interesting: the theater at Whitehall, after 1605, was arranged so that Charles I was seated at the exact center of the hall. He, along with the other royal spectators, was a part of the show – the theater remained lit during performances – and the audience was integrated into the symbolic action of the masque at its dramatic climax. The Stuart court masque, as Stephen Orgel shows, was designed as a ritual celebration of the power and splendor of the court hierarchy. But note that geometry, in the service of political absolutism, places the monarch exactly opposite the vanishing point of the perspective setting on the backdrop of the stage. It is as though the royal identity and its hidden destiny were most fully manifest in this unconsciously contrived correspondence of

passage dominated by the solar eye, like the stanza in which the nymph is invoked by her whiteness (46), is a focus of light, but while the light of Galatea is manifold, a galaxy or a texture of illumination, the Cyclopean light is insistently, purposively focused – like the lamp on a miner's forehead, a light designed to disclose and extract. The various light of the nymph is suggested by the repeated image of the peacock, whose mythical origin is the hundred-eyed Argus. The many-eyed plumage of the bird is in turn the night sky, "el celestial zafiro." The poem inclines westward, tracing the course of solar light, and ends with its displacement by nocturnal, lunar light, the silver light of the poet – Yeats' lunar light, or Pound's art of the silversmith, favored by Artemis. This aesthetic light is the light of beings who are poised gracefully between seeing and being seen: such a being is Acis, who, watched by the admiring Galatea, feigns sleep but tactfully watches the nymph in turn, with the hundred eyes of the peacock. In the realm of *Aphros* eyes – figures of light on a blue field, of plumage or sky – are more than organs of perception, for like flowers or stars they too appear and have their place in the aesthetic order of the cosmos, and in the heraldry of the imagination. They reflect and are seen, oblivious of the Cyclopean claim to be a pure perceiving subject, and exclusive arbiter of the order of things.

---

opposites: absolute royal power and the vortex of receding space which is the vortex of the king's own imminent oblivion. The landscape perspective of baroque painting and garden design implants a point of corrosion in an otherwise contained space, imposing a consciousness not only of distance but of irreversible change.

CHAPTER III

SATURN AND VENUS

> "If we were to philosophize (a little), we might say that the being of things is not in their heaviness but in their lightness; which would perhaps confirm Nietzsche's proposition: 'what is good is light.'"
>
> Roland Barthes

1. SATURNINE MELANCHOLY AND THE VENUSIAN REALM

The Saturnine type, according to Ficino, is one of the "separated ones," submerged in subjectivity, capable of both genius and brutishness; sublimity and barbarism. One of the motives of Ficino's work on melancholy in *De vita triplici* was a strategy of planetary counter-influences to the negative effects of the black bile of Saturn. Three planets are offered as antidotes: Sol, Jupiter and Venus. Of these Venus was believed to be the most inimical to Saturn, exerting an allure which would draw the afflicted soul away from the dark center of self towards the external world and engagement with the other. The Neoplatonist Ficino, a strong advocate of the positive power of images in the soul, devised an archetypal and aesthetic therapy whereby Venusian influence could be transmitted to the afflicted psyche. The benefit might bestowed by images of the goddess herself, or through proximity to substances or colors associated with her, such as gardens and meadows, greenness and water. (20,62) Through the attracting force of these images of beauty and fertility, which might be experienced either directly or through the decor of a room carefully designed for this therapeutic purpose, the victim of melancholy would be lured back into the world of the senses and restored to whatever psychic balance was possible to an irremediably fallen condition.

Ficino, who thought of himself (not without some pride) as a melancholy type, imagined the overcoming of melancholy as a centrifugal movement of the soul away from darkness towards light – the light at the circumference which distracts the brooding self from its own engulfing depth. The idea of Venus and feminine beauty as a beneficent distraction places Ficino in direct opposition to the Hesiodic tradition of the "curse" of the feminine. In the *Theogony* Aphrodite arises as the primeval type of malign erotic seduction; the "historical" correlative of her birth is Zeus's revenge on Prometheus and the entire "race" of men by means of the creation of the first woman:

> In return for the theft of fire he instantly produced a curse to plague mankind. At the orders of the son of Cronus, the famous lame smith-god shaped some clay in the image of a tender girl. The bright-eyed goddess Athena dressed and decked her in silvery clothes. A marvelous embroidered veil fell from her head and was held in her hands. Round her head the goddess tied a golden diadem on which smith-god himself had exercised his skill, to please his father Zeus. When Zeus had completed this beautiful curse to go with the blessing of fire, he displayed the girl in an assembly of gods and men, all decked out in the finery supplied by the bright-eyed daughter of the lord of hosts. Gods and men were speechless when they saw how deadly and how irresistible was the trick with which Zeus was going to catch mankind.
>
> This was the origin of the damnable race of women – a plague which men must live with. (Brown 69)

The same myth appears in *Works and Days* in the story of Pandora, whose name means "the gift of all" and who was devised by the collaborating gods as a punitive gift to men. As in the Biblical story of the Fall, the human race is sentenced to hard labor by a god seeking to punish disobedience. In return for the theft of fire Zeus retaliates with the inner fire of erotic love, the plague brought by Pandora, who is endowed with a deceitful tongue and treacherous ways. (Pandora releases a swarm of afflictions from a great jar [*pithos*, normally used to store grain.])

In the Hesiodic tradition the beauty of Venus is a deadly mirage with the power to disarm the hero. The story of Venus and Mars provides the archetype for male susceptibility to the "gaze" of feminine beauty, which renders him passive and vulnerable. Milton's god, like Hesiod's Zeus, plants a lure and trap for his Adam by placing before him a figure of supreme beauty and desirability. And as Adam describes his first encounter with Eve to Raphael, he confesses his feelings of self-doubt:

> ... in all enjoyments else
> Superior and unmov'd, here only weak
> Against the charm of Beauty's powerful glance.
> (VIII.531-33)

Beauty here is active and dangerous; it asserts itself as a *regard*, a glance which penetrates the armor of the Adamic ego. Eve seems to the uninitiated Adam consummate, complete — the pinnacle of God's creation: "As one intended / First, not after / Made." (555)[1]

Milton's Adam vacillates between awe of Eve's beauty and seemingly superior form, and his astute suspicion that she is essentially flawed — her finer appearance concealing some inner deficiency — since her beauty makes him feel weak. And Raphael confirms his doubts about his too-dazzling spouse, advising him, rather in the manner of a village priest counseling a parishioner burdened with a troublesome wife, to assert his authority: "the more she will acknowledge thee her Head, / And to realities yield all her shows;" The proper placement of Eve in relation to Adam depends on Adam's recognition that her appearance belongs to the realm of "unreality." For Eve is not only secondary and deficient in her being; she is a less real version of the prototype, who is in turn an image of his creator. A chain of de-substantialization is proposed, from God to Adam to Eve; for while Adam is the original of his race, and has a direct line to Reality, having been made in God's image, Eve is but an image of an image. She is

---

[1] In a reversal of this situation in which man is the victim of active, provocative feminine beauty, Góngora attributes this power and allure to the figure of Acis. As Galatea watches him, his active physical attraction becomes a serpent whose venom Galatea longs to drink. (St. 36) Her former "monstruo de rigor," the monstrous rigor of her chastity, is defeated by the sensuous atmosphere of the bower and by the "rhetorical silence" of Acis' virile beauty.

metaphysically declassé, marginal, slippery, vagrant: an appearance, with the capacity of mere appearances to bedazzle and deceive. History will devolve from Adam's entanglement therein.[2]

Góngora, Milton's contemporary, inclines towards the other tradition, one that recognizes the value in what Nietzsche was to call "the consciousness of appearance" (*The Gay Science* 116) and for which appearance is not that which veils the truth, but simply "that which lives."[3] Ficino's theraphy of images proposes that the victim of melancholy needs, above all, to be distracted from himself, and even willingly deceived by the world of appearances, captivated by the suspected possibilities in life. Without this program of self-overcoming, the world-rejecting inner self, starved of images, is experienced as a kind of death. Ficino's Venus, "She who enraptures the eye," sponsors the attracting surfaces of things, which in themselves possess soul, because "There is nothing so deformed in the whole living world that it has no soul, no gift of soul contained in it." (87) Insofar as she moves the self back to an awareness of its physical, perceiving, and imagining existence she is a challenge to the arrogance of subjectivism and to fantasies of disembodied thought and existence which appear, in the Spanish baroque, in violent counterpoint to *Gongorismo* and the "Italianate" influence.

Saturn, on the other hand, moves the soul to contract into itself, exerting his tyranny at the opaque center of self, pulling his victim away from Venusian stimuli and relegating those distracting phenomena to the category of illusory, transient, and deceptive. It is in fact Saturn who is behind all philosophies which pose a single truth against manifold reality, and who lurks behind the views,

---

[2] As Jean Rousset remarks of the undulating facades of baroque architecture, that they are renaissance facades seen as though through water, "plongées dans l'eau," (157) so is Eve to Adam: baroque and undulating, seen through a moving screen of water, an unsettled and unsettling version of the original, normative structure.

[3] More recently the zoologist Adolf Portmann, citing the "functionless characteristics" of many natural forms, proposes that we designate "the entire universe of form-phenomena" as "self-presentation" and accept the value of the facade and its difference from the hidden inner structures of things. Portmann in fact links his anti-classical view of natural form with "mannerism" – that way of looking at things which makes "breaches into another world," a world in which beauty, in Rilke's words, may be "the beginning of the terrible" rather than a revelation of the rationality of nature. (27-38)

whether Hesiodic or Miltonic, of woman as insubstantial "show," etc. It is the elderly ascetic Critilo in Gracián's *Criticón* who plays the Saturnine role of undeceiving mentor, imposing the Stoic habit of *nil admirari* on his young charge. (This very task of grim instruction may in itself have served a therapeutic purpose for the sage, who is stimulated to action by the challenge of doing battle with Gracián's Felliniesque carnival world.)

It is important to recognize that the Saturn-Venus relationship I have sketched here has a symbolic antecedent in Hesiod's story of Aphrodite's birth. The seemingly baroque juxtaposition of monstrosity and beauty so often cited in relation to the poem is anticipated in the circumstances of Aphrodite's birth in the *Theogony*: Kronos' castration of his father Ouranos is the immediate cause of her coming into being; the goddess of beauty arises as the consequence of this cosmic act of savagery, rising from the white *aphros* which issues from the severed organs of the god. Out of the brutal act of mutilation by the sickle-wielding Kronos comes the beautiful white-skinned goddess with "delicate feet," attended by Eros and Himnos (desire). Her generation is violent, but quickly transformed into an image of supreme beauty; this affirmation of form contains the seeds of the Ovidian metamorphosis of Acis following upon the volcanic eruption of Cyclopean violence. And in fact the myth of Aphrodite is the prototype in Mediterranean culture of all subsequent conjunctions of beauty and violence, or beauty and monstrosity, and a paradigm for aestheticism, or the will-to-form as an *emergence* from darkness, violence, and incoherence.

In Hesiod's account the goddess is identified first by her whiteness: ". . . Then white foam issued from the divine flesh, and in the foam a girl began to grow." (Brown 58) She touches earth first at Kythera (an alternate name for Aphrodite) and then at Kypros: "There she stepped out, a goddess, tender and beautiful, and round her slender feet the green grass shot up." (Brown 58) This attention given to the goddess's feet reappears in Góngora's poem in the Cyclops' fantasy of his nymph: in Stanza 47 Polyphemus imagines that when Galatea steps from the sea onto sand, the magical contact of her white feet with the shells will effect a spontaneous generation of pearls:

> Pisa la arena, que en la arena adoro
> cuantas el blanco pie conchas platea,
> cuyo bello contacto puede hacerlas,
> sin concebir rocío, parir perlas.
>
> (373-76)

> [Walk on the beach, that I may there admire
> How shells beneath your feet to silver turn,
> From which made fruitful by your shining tread,
> Without conceiving dewdrops, pearls are bred.]

This passage belongs to a pattern of images in which an agent associated with the sea and its generative power transforms the surface of things. The foaming Sicilian sea (l. 26), Galatea's feet (l. 374), the transformed blood of Acis, engender new surfaces in cliffs, shells, sand and tree-roots. The dominant color in these events is silver-white, a mineralized *aphros*, the aesthetic substance which illumines the surface of the world and subverts the *melancólico vacío*.

Where Nietzsche, in *The Birth of Tragedy*, saw the relationship of monstrosity and beauty in terms of the historical movement from Dionysian origin to Apollonian sublimation, we are concerned here less with a process than with a perpetual state of tension between the two.[4] Venus always has a shadow in Saturn, in the form of withdrawal, inwardness, the threat of inundating depths, monstrous subjectivity. In the same way, poetic activity is always shadowed by the speechlessness of the poet's melancholy submersion in his own psychic depths, which may be experienced as a devouring monster who suppresses the birth of articulate language. The underworld is an ever-present threat to aesthetic activity, like Hades lurking beneath the meadows of Persephone and Eurydice. Conversely, poetic creation may proceed from inner violence and darkness, and Góngora's Cyclops functions as the poet's mask in this respect, the poet who in his "soledad confusa," the chaos of his

---

[4] For Nietzsche the monstrous consists of the nihilism which distorts life deprived of the illusions provided by artistic form. Art is more enhancing to life than truth. The fixation (*verfestigung*) upon metaphysical truth impedes the flow of becoming by denying the chaos attendant upon true thinking and the truths which may arise from it. See David Farrell Krell, "Art and Truth in Raging Discord: Heidegger and Nietzsche on the Will to Power." (38-52)

solitude, gives birth to the mirage of Galatea and her entire Venusian realm of beauty.

The dark and Saturnine presence of the Cyclops in the pastoral landscape threatens a schism between objective surface and subjective depth, for his dissonant presence forces the coming into being of these categories, and forces them apart. The echoes of his barbarous pipes, composed of one hundred reeds, alters, "altera," the environment drastically, causing confusion and fear in nature:

> La selva se confunde el mar se altera,
> rompe Tritón su caracol torcido,
> sordo huye el bajel a vela y remo:
> ¡tal la música es de Polifemo!
> (St. 12)

> [The tree-tops toss, the surges crash and grind,
> His trump of twisted nacre Triton breaks,
> Fear wings with sail or oar the deafened boats:
> So barbarous are Polyphemus' notes!

We may profitably compare the opacity and dense profundity of the Cyclopean realm relative to the translucent surfaces of the "reino de la espuma" to Gille Deleuze's juxtaposition of Lewis Carroll and Antonin Artaud. Deleuze remarks that the most significant of Alice's adventures in Wonderland is in fact her eventual rise to the surface and triumph over the nonsense world of depth. (*Logique du sens* 114) In her buoyancy and apparent fragility, and in her suspension between childhood and womanhood, the young girl, represented by Alice and other nymph-like creatures of fiction and myth, is a kind of floating, almost incorporeal being, a creature of surfaces. The Greeks acknowledged her precariously gliding quality in such *kore* as Persephone and Eurydice, whose floral, ephemeral natures are menaced by the rapacious depths of Hades. The *kore* embody a delicate, transient beauty which is always theatened by the devouring abyss concealed beneath the apparent innocence of spring meadows. Carroll, as we know, was captivated by this moment in the life of the female child in which she is suspended, as Deleuze sees it, between the maternal depths which she has shed and the discovery of the depths of her own physical being. This pause in the life of the young girl is a *court moment de surface* in which she seems to glide over water, like Alice in the pool of her own tears. (114)

Artaud and his linguistic experiments are offered as an example of a radical revulsion from surface phenomena (he in fact wrote a violent critique of Carroll), as manifested in his efforts to reduce language to non-sense by corporealizing it: linguistic articulation was to be defeated by *ingestion*, the language of the body. In posing the truth of the body and of matter against the immateriality of language, Artaud reverses the metaphysical hierarchy, and so remains within it (a charge Heidegger would make of Nietzschean deconstruction), a victim of its debris. *Parler* becomes *manger*, and discourse is held subject to the "god of the cave." The poet has become an ogre, devouring his own medium. Here language as Saturnine discourse is carried to its extreme: Valéry's dictum, "le plus profond, c'est la peau" inverted in a fantasy of the body as an absorbing depth unprotected by skin. In his vehement opposition to surface phenomena Artaud embodies the recoil from the *via aesthetica*, the way of sensing, of allowing for the unsolicited presence of things. Carried to its logical extreme the monistic enthrallment with depth results in the complete abolition of linguistic form, and in fact Artaud experimented with a poetic language liberated from semantic and phonetic sense – a non-sense language. Depth of meaning is deepened to un-meaning.

Polyphemus follows the reverse procedure, moving from the inarticulate depth of the body to linguistic engagement with the world, clumsily acknowledging the primacy of the aesthetic in human existence. And despite the Cyclopean destruction of the bower the dominant movement in Góngora's poem is not one of ingestion and destruction but of gliding and efflorescence; this last, extravagant flowering of Cyclopean pastoral resolves itself in the creation of sense from the non-sense of Cyclopean violence and the Saturnine melancholy long associated with the depths of the earth. The sovereignty of the ephemeral nymph implies, in its *affleuver*, a universe irreducible in its mobility and in its plurality of worlds. Its values, other than beauty, are correspondence, relation, association; things are interwoven, entangled, enthralled.

2. Cyclopean Song

Many of Góngora's contemporaries found his long poems not only enigmatic but chaotic and godless, a bewildering maze of thought and impression. They were fashioned to confound, entangle and lead astray towards the heterodox cult of beauty. Both poets of the *Polifemo*, "culto" and "bárbaro", worship at the altar of beauty, which is indifferent to, or in recoil from, desire. As I noted briefly in Chapter II, the verb *adora* in Stanza 13 marks the pivot whereby Saturn is placed in contact with Venus, and the prison-like *caverna profunda* opens out onto a luminous landscape. Góngora moves us from the barbarism of Cyclopean pipe music to the theme of the nymph and her realm, the "reino de la espuma." The Cyclops has so far been presented as a savage submerged in darkness and solitude, then a monstrous proprietor, a hunter, a greedy harvester of fruits and nuts, and finally rustic musician whose pipes terrify all of nature. In the passage which introduces the Galatea theme, his savagery and gigantism, through the act of adoration of an ideal being, become submerged, immersed in the "reino de la espuma."

> Ninfa, de Doris hija, la más bella,
> adora, que vio el reino de la espuma.
> Galatea es su nombre, y dulce en ella
> el terno Venus de sus Gracias suma.
> Son una y otra luminosa estrella
> lucientes ojos de su blanca pluma:
> si roca de cristal no es de Neptuno,
> pavón de Venus es, cisne de Juno.
>
> (St. 13)

> [He loves a nymph, daughter of Doris, fair
> Above all seen in ocean's kingdom yet;
> Her name is Galatea, and in her
> Of Venus' Graces all the charms are met.
> Bright stars, both one and other, are the pair
> Of shining eyes in snow-white plumage set:
> If not a rock of crystal in the sea,
> Then Juno's swan or Venus' peacock she.]

The passage depicts the movement of the self outwards in the act of adoration. The verb *adora*, first of all, is the interloping term that dislocates, as hyperbaton (l. *transgressio*, called by Puttenham the "overreacher" in the *Arte of English poesie*, 1589) it interferes with the sense of "Ninfa, de Doris hija, la más bella que vio el reino de la espuma," forcing the reader to "step across" the intrusion in order to re-compose the figure of the nymph as a superlative being within her realm of water and spume. At the same time, Polyphemus is present only in this predicate, whose subordinate clause unfolds an entire universe of meaning: "el reino de la espuma." The meaning which is disrupted becomes a net into which the hyperbaton and its perpetrator are interwoven, and the Cyclops, detached from any defining pronoun, is engulfed by the radiant object of his desire, the direct object "ninfa," and the subordinate clause which stands for the nymph's mother and their mutual territory, the realm of *aphros*.

Stanza 46, which begins Polyphemus' song to Galatea, recapitulates the narrator's lines of Stanza 13, rephrasing in a direct address to the nymph the earlier description of Galatea, with its stress on whiteness, luminousness, and its allusions to the birds of Juno and Venus, the swan and the peacock. After the barbarous prelude of Polyphemus' bagpipes, the second voice of the poem steps forward:

> Oh bella Galatea, más suave
> que los claveles que tronchó la aurora;
> blanca más que las plumas de aquel ave
> que dulce muere y en las aguas mora;
> igual en pompa al pájaro que, grave,
> su manto azul de tantos ojos dora
> cuantas el celestial zafiro estrellas!
> ¡Oh tú, que en dos incluyes las más bellas!
>
> [Fair maiden, gentler than a flower bent low
> When dawn's first dewdrop on its petals lies,
> With plumage whiter than the swan can show,
> Who dwells upon the sea, and singing dies
> Splendid as the peacock, for although
> His azure mantle shines with golden eyes
> Thick as the stars that stud the sapphire zone,
> No two are lovelier, maiden, than your own.]

In his own song Polyphemus acts out the verb *adora* which had characterized him in the earlier stanza. And in conjuring forth the absent Galatea he conforms to the narrator's own metaphors: the nymph is the whiteness of lilies and swan, her splendor and bright eyes are like the eyes which adorn the peacock's feathers. As an articulation of desire the song makes a bridge between the "dolor interno" of the cavern and the external world onto which the Cyclops projects the turbulence of his monstrous depths. It also mediates between two silences: the silence of the indifferent divinities of nature, including the nymph herself, and the silence of the Cyclopean *dolor,* the suffering inwardness that precedes the song. The silence which precedes song, both the Cyclopean lament and the poet's own verse, is conspicuous. The first silence is requested by the poet, who calls upon his patron, the Duke of Niebla, to attend to the poet's own music – "son de la zampoña mía" – and that of his giant, "de músico jayán el fiero canto." The reader is prepared by these pauses for each movement into lyrical language, of the finer pastoral of the narrator, and of the "fiero canto," or fierce song, of the Cyclops; and the stress given to silence in each case serves to heighten the self-consciousness of language.

The Dedication to the poem leads the reader to anticipate the enclosure of the Cyclops' rustic song (stanzas 46-58) within the finer music of the poem. The rustic, bucolic content of the tale will be dignified by a *culto,* or elevated style. The verb *escuchar,* to listen, occurs twice in the three dedicatory stanzas: First as an imperative: "escucha, al son de la zampoña mía," as the poet asks his patron for attention, hoping to distract him from the pleasures of the hunt (6); then in 19-20, in the indicative mood, as the Duke is now portrayed, having abandoned the hunt at the poet's request, seated and waiting for Cyclopean song to commence (in Cunningham's translation "to listen" returns to the imperative): ". . . en cuanto / debajo escuchas de dosel augusto, / del músico jayán el fiero canto." ". . . listen in state / From your high seat, while now the barbarous measure / Of the gigantic bard I celebrate." I propose that we consider this enclosed, fiercer music, the object of "escuchas," as the voice of Góngora himself, in buffoonish disguise, as he pays tribute to the source of his inspiration, Venus. His own unreconstructed monster, his inwardness, is the model for the ruder song of alienation, longing, resentment, and desire and it is enclosed within "la zampoña mía," the finer, finished product. Polyphemus' song is poet's dedication of the *selva oscura* of his inner self to the praise of beauty. Cyclopean song confirms the adoration attributed to the giant in Stanza 13, voicing a mute adoration and, temporarily at least, subduing monstrous depths by the articulation of illusion, moving attention away from the center of self *(caverna)* to the periphery *(reino de la espuma)*.

Primitive force, personified in early Greek mythology in titans and ogres, is here harnessed to poetic creation. Instead of swallowing the world, Polyphemus bows before its divinity in the form of his fantasy of Galatea. Light, motion, fluidity: these are the essential components of his fantasy, notably alien to his experience. They are also the visually captivating phenomena which the Greeks personified in naiads. Polyphemus creates, like his author, out of an abysmal solitude, emerging from his melancholy void to contemplate the play of light on water, the visual spectacle celebrated by the Greeks which diverts consciousness from its depths, beguiling it with moving, shimmering light.

Ficino writes in *De vita triplici* (93) that when Pythagorean maguses became melancholy and torpid from too much cogitation they donned white garments and proceeded to sing and play music, thereby consorting with the creative, expansive powers of Jove and Apollo and prolonging their lives. Polyphemus' song is such a Ficinian rehabilitation of the melancholy self through immersion in whiteness and light. It is notable that while Polyphemus' opening lines are based on the poet's own description of Galatea, the aura of whiteness is intensified over the white of the prior lines. While the white of the narrator's lines is intermingled with the crimson of roses, "o púrpura nevada, o nieve roja," the singer focuses intently upon the pure white light of his fantasy, employing the comparative "blanca más" and linking this attribute to a divine power of transformation, which is the power to create more light:

> Deja las ondas, deja el rubio coro
> de las hijas de Tetis, ya el mar vea,
> cuando niega la luz un carro de oro,
> que en dos la restituye Galatea.
> Pisa la arena, que en la arena adoro
> cuantas el blanco pie conchas platea

cuyo bello contacto puede hacerlas,
sin concebir rocío, parir perlas.

(St. 47)

[Forsake the waves, forsake the bright-haired choir
Of Tethys' daughters, and the waves shall learn,
When not lit by a car of golden fire,
That Galatea's eyes as brightly burn.
Walk on the beach, that I may there admire
How shells beneath your feet to silver turn,
From which, made fuitful by your shining tread,
Without conceiving dewdrops, pearl are bred.]

The imagery in Polyphemus' praise of Galatea centers on eyes and on variations of vision and light. In his plea to her to leave the ocean he imagines that the sea will "see" ("el mar vea," "let the ocean see") the restoration of the dying light in her eyes: "en dos la restituye Galatea." (372) The two suns of the nymph's eyes will bring back the light which is erased by the chariot of Helios as it descends into the void of the west – "cuando niega la luz un carro de oro" (371) – a paradoxical figure which shows light effaced by the golden radiance of the chariot. Melancholy is overcome, and the beauty of the world is distilled into images of light, especially in the fantasy of the loved one as generative light. Polyphemus' song has two centers of awareness, that of the self (goatherd, afflicted lover, musician, god) and that of the beloved, and each of these nuclei is a concentration of light, captured optically as though the Cyclops' eye could condense all of the meaning of the world, contain and reflect it.

While the eye-star-sun conceits are part of the inherited conventions of love poetry, it is worth examining these images more closely in view of the importance Góngora accords optical experience. In the first stanzas of Polyphemus' song meaning is distilled in figures of vision and in the sequence of points of light and whiteness: stars – peacock eyes – eyes of nymph – gold chariot – sunlight – eyes – white feet – pearls. And this concentration of meaning in light and vision occurs again in the Cyclops' self-description in Stanza 53 of his song. Here he creates a myth of the self, a fantasy of a solar, divine identity which is a source of light and vision. This mythological self includes everything else, casting its sovereign illumination over world and nymph, who is urged not to hide from the terrible Helios-like gaze of her admirer: "Polifemo te llama, no te escondas;" (405) and to admire his prodigious figure. His song develops a kind of double mirage of both the self and the other, and culminates in this scene of self-hypnosis. We see him, in Stanza 53, as he sees himself, a mythological, solar self, a celestial being whose radiance is mirrored in the compliant sea.

But while the element of water plays a neutral and passive role in Cyclopean apotheosis — the moment when he is revealed to himself as a god — it otherwise has an active and transforming role in the poem, as *aphros*. And what we find interwoven into this story is a kind of dance of elemental powers or cosmic principles: one, the sea, is a community of divinities, who flee at the sound of Polyphemus' music and whom Galatea calls on to save Acis. The other, the sun, whose divinity is manifested briefly in the figure of Polyphemus, is singular and fixed in the sky like a single eye. The solar light projects the sense of an integrated identity, a reassuring, centralized focus: I am this person who loves that person who is thus and thus; water, on the other hand, is the element of metamorphosis, of identity in flux and change. And solar light is tied to a cycle, and is about to be received, as the chariot of Helios, into the western sea. (St. 43) In Góngora's polytheistic scheme divinity manifests itself as a plurality of changing forms, and the omnipotence of one deity is shown to be a delusion.

Polyphemus is not so engrossed in his images of Galatea that he abandons his narcissism, and the song is not only an objectification of his love-melancholy, but a gesture of denial of the tragic self, of the self as abyss. The day is dying, as the light of the sun sinks into the ocean, and the rustic song is an attempt to hold back the coming dark with its points of light, its immutable images of beauty and light. The incoherence of the singer's earthliness becomes, precariously, a world. The yearning movement of the psyche towards surface and light also generates images of wholeness, focus, and restoration — the loved one has the power to restore a broken, incomplete world as well as to hold back the dark; at the same time she can bring into being new worlds of light, distilled in the pearls which will come into being as her feet touch down on the sand and shells of the beach. If she would respond to his pleas, the Cyclopean world would be transformed; light would return, civilization would commence, the cave will be illumined.

The conclusion of Polyphemus' song, its breaking off at the interruption of the vine-trampling goats (impious to Bacchus as Polyphemus is to the other gods), and its failure to entirely dispel the *dolor interno* (St. 59) points to the limits of lyrical and aesthetic experience and its power to defeat the tragic awareness of the *caverna profunda*. The cavern, concealed by the gagged mouth of the cave, is nonetheless disclosed in the act of singing, whereby consciousness reverberates outwards into space, dissolving its density in a boundless atmosphere. As in a painting by Rembrandt, the substance – in this case the mineral-like substance of Cyclopean identity – yields to space and atmosphere. *Dolor interno* has been given a surface, a place in the world as musical form and as the poetry which transcribes it. What was within is now without.

The structure of the song which projects Cyclopean desire towards the fear, disdain, and rejection of the nymph unfolds in five parts:

1) Praise of Galatea (361-368)
2) Pleas to Galatea (369-384)
   to hear his song
   to abandon the sea
3) Self-praise (385-424)
   possessions
   lineage
   stature/looks
4) Autobiography (425-460)
   former savage habits and current civility
   narration of the shipwrecked Genoan
5) Renewed pleas and offering of gifts (461-464)

After beginning with the exclamatory "Oh bella Galatea" the song moves into convolution; memory complicates the song of praise, adorning it with the reorganized past of the convert. Love, so the giant tells Galatea, has refined him: he is no longer the loutish and greedy cannibal of Homer and Euripides but "por tu causa," (431), "because of you," a civil, courteous host, his cave no longer a macabre gallery of human heads but a hostel for shipwrecked wanderers. The song, although rustic in style, offers evidence of a move towards refinement, modifying the earlier picture of the "fiero jayán," the pine-tree wielding goatherd-hunter of mountainous body and Lethean hair. He describes his pipe music as "yugo bien suave," a "gentle yoke," in contrast to the narrator's earlier description of a terrifying blast of sound. And as Polyphemus sees it, it is the *sea* which is fierce ("fiero mar") rather than his music, which is gentle and Orphic. He invites the nymph to move into the orbit of his civility; he proposes to rescue her from a world where shellfish emit grotesque music (381-382) and storms shatter sailing ships (433-436), and to provide in exchange his own pastoral world of peaceful abundance and order. He imagines cosmic powers for his music, comically unaware that its effects are similar (like a terrible storm of sound) to the disorder it is meant to displace:

>Yugo aquel día, y yugo bien süave,
>del fiero mar a la sañuda frente
>imponiéndole estaba (si no al viento
>dulcísimas coyundas) mi instrumento,
>
>(433-440)

>[While with its yoke that day my instrument
>An easy yoke indeed, strove to command
>The stubborn forehead of the angry seas,
>Or with still gentler chains to bind the breeze,]

Polyphemus is in fact a savage whose unsettling excursion into lyrical language renders him even more monstrous. His language alters the landscape, just as Acis' blood will "silver" over the tree-roots and sand in the final *octava*. The latter event harmonizes and resolves, while the former acts as an aggressive dissonance, a rude interruption into the natural world of *selva, mar, cavernas* and *ribazos*. In Stanza 49 in which the essential distress of his language becomes the material of his own metaphor, tears are compared to rivers and goat's milk – the goats' epic thirst may empty the rivers, but their milk and his tears continue to flow:

>'Pastor soy, mas tan rico de ganados,
>que los valles impido mas vacíos,
>los cerros desparezco levantados,

y los caudales seco de los ríos:
no los que, de sus ubres desatados
o derribados de los ojos míos,
leche corren y lágrimas; que iguales
en número a mis bienes son mis males.

[A shepherd I, with flocks so well supplied
They hide the mountain tops, however high;
They fill the valley beds, however wide;
The largest river, when they drink, runs dry.
Not so the streams that from their udders glide,
Nor those that draw their waters from my eye –
Torrents of milk and tears, whose volume shows
My goods are matched in number by my woes.]

As a disruption of cosmic silence language functions as negation, a negation proceeding from melancholy. Cyclopean song falls like a violent storm over the island, (already alerted by the terrible prelude of the giant's *zampoña*), and violently severs humanity from nature. Its thundering sound is announced twice: in line 359, "el trueno de la voz," and again when the Cyclops spies the lovers fleeing the shattered bower

y al garzón viendo, cuantas mover pudo
celoso trueno, antiguas hayas mueve:
tal, antes que la opaca nube rompa,
previene rayo fulminante trompa.
(485-488)

[While Acis followed, never storm displaced
So many beech-trees as his jealous roar;
Thus thunder sounds its warning trumpet loud
Before the bolt bursts from a gloomy cloud.]

Thunder makes a link between Cyclopean song and violence, marking first its eruption, and then its degeneration into a roar of rage.

3. Venus and the "reino de la espuma"

I remarked above that for Ficino's melancholic "separated ones" the power of Venus is the beneficent lure to external things, while the Hesiodic tradition views entanglement in feminine wiles as one of the chief misfortunes of mankind. The Ficinian idea of this Venusian pull towards the surface is, like Dámaso Alonso's characterization of *gongorismo*, a *movimiento hacia afuera*, an enthrallment which is not entrapment but a movement of the psyche towards a fruitful engagement with the world. The realm of Venus is the "reino de la espuma," the community of sea-deities whose field of creation is *aphros, espuma,* sea-spume.[5] The goddess, as reigning deity of the island and of the poem, sponsors the activity of creative disclosure, by which the boundaries of illusion are expanded, appearances multiplied by the silver mirrors of aestheticism and given a buoyancy which makes them seem timeless, rootless, viewed from the perspective of the timebound subjectivity of the *caverna*.

Just as Góngora's Cyclops is cast in a shape whose history reaches back beyond Ovid's Hellenistic poem and its pastoral antecedents to the ogres of folklore and epic, the figure of the nymph Galatea is informed by repeated associations with Venus and Aphrodite. That Galatea is in fact a synecdoche for the goddess is supported by the numerous references to Venusian symbols and themes: sea-spume, the dove and the swan, cult places such as Pafo and Gnidus, roses and lilies, the myrtle. Sicily itself, which worships Galatea as goddess of the harvest, was the site of a famous sanctuary, Mt. Eryx (Erice) in the northwest part of the island not far from the peninsula whose ancient name was Lilybaeum.

In addition to the many Venusian symbols scattered throughout the verses dedicated to the Galatea theme, there is another, little-noticed but significant attribute which links the nymph to the Aphrodite of the *Theogony*. After being introduced by the narrator as the daughter of Doris and Nereus, she is depicted gliding from

---

[5] John Beverley notes that the rhyme "pluma"-"espuma" signifies the presence of Venus at several points throughout the *Soledades*. (31)

sea to shore, pursued by Glaucus and Palaemon. The fact that her altar, as we are told, is on the shore – "el margen donde para su pie ligera" – makes her a creature of boundaries; she spans two realms, as though she were an amphibious being. This gliding movement between two kinds of space (and both Góngora's long poems show that the boundary between sea and land fascinated the poet) reinforces Galatea's Venusian identity at a deeper level of meaning than do the more commonly invoked symbols such as the dove and the myrtle. Moreover, Polyphemus' fantasy of the nymph includes a half-articulate longing, originating in Theocritus, for a kind of union between sea and earth. If Galatea will only leave the sea and step onto land (since he cannot move in the opposite direction): light will be restored, shells will become pearls, Galatea will be both a Venus of the sea and a Cupid in the mountains, brandishing the bow and quiver bestowed upon her suitor by the grateful shipwrecked Genoan. (St. 58)

Polyphemus' vision of the world as it will be when Galatea comes to earth is a matter not only of restored light but of wholeness: the union of two spheres whose rupture has traditionally vexed him. If she will "evolve" onto land, then his own landlocked condition will not seem a deficiency. The sea is alien territory to the Cyclops, a rival whose coral and shellfish are obstacles, keeping Galatea from hearing his pleas. (St. 48) At the same time the Cyclops boasts of his marine parentage: Even though he is a shepherd, his father is Neptune, monarch of the deep sea caves, and Galatea stands to gain an imposing father-in-law if she concedes to wed the giant:

> 'Del Júpiter soy hijo, de las ondas,
> aunque pastor; si tu desdén no espera
> a que el monarca de esas grutas hondas,
> en trono de cristal te abrace nuera,
>
> (401-404)

> ['Though but a shepherd, he who rules the waves
> Sired me, so if you wait not in your pride
> Till, on his crystal throne in ocean's caves,
> Neptune himself shall kiss you as my bride,]

Paul Friederich writes that the island sites of Aphrodite's cult – Cyprus, Sicily, Cythera, and Crete suggest "liminality," "interstitial and marginal states and processes," (132-149) and argues that Aphrodite symbolizes a "crossing over" between emotional antitheses, and that her power is manifested "betwixt and between" stable structures and categories of reality. Galatea's marginality, and the tension between the two realms which Polyphemus imagines he will resolve if she will only step onto shore, suggest the nymph's participation in this aspect of Venusian power and meaning. Although I have preferred the term amphibianism to denote this phenomenon of marginal and mediating states, Friederich's ideas on the subject are sufficiently pertinent to my thesis and suggestive in their cultural implications for me to refer briefly to some of them here. He offers several examples of images which refer to the mediating role of the goddess: sea-foam, a substance which arises between air and water; water birds, and the insularity of her cult – islands being a type of *temenos*, a space marked off for the use of a god. (70)[6]

When posed against solar divinity this goddess of marginal states seems elusive. The power of Helios is intensely focused, and is an obvious analogue for the One as opposed to the Many, a duality which first appeared in pre-Socratic though and became a cornerstone of western metaphysics. At the same time, this solar power is fixed and circumscribed by the boundaries of sea, earth, and night. (*Heraclitus Seminar* 168) Galatea, as "fugitiva ninfa" and "fugitiva nieve" is a mobile deity whose characteristic movement of *circulation* sharply contrasts with Cyclopean fixedness, the pronounced, emphatic ego-state which requires clearly defined boundaries and which styles itself "árbitro de montañas y ribera." In the portrayal of the giant's towering helplessness as he gazes out towards the sea he will never navigate, there is an echo of the blinded Homeric Cyclops trying to make out his target by the sound of the departing Odysseus' mocking voice. Other beings are always arriving and departing, but Polyphemus will never leave his

---

[6] The marginality of Venus is also the marginality of the feminine, which is both a defined category (as aberration or deviancy) and, as the unknowable other, that which escapes conceptualization. The position of Eve on the scale of beings is problematic, caught as it is in hesitation between the party of God and Adam (essence) and the party of nature (appearance).

cave and his cliff, finding consolation only in his own dazzling image and in the gratifications of prodigious ownership.

In terms, then, of their characteristic gestures, the mode of Galatea is one of moving through the world, while the Cyclopean mode gathers in the world, objectifying and devouring it. The *glissando* of nymphs leaves the world, except for the hearts of rejected suitors, intact, and in fact participates in the essential fluidity of reality free from the optical and linguistic devices of containment and definition employed by the human will. It operates, this gliding movement, in fundamental ignorance of the device of boundaries, the arbitrary, space-determining boundaries which are a part of Cyclopean ego equipment. The nymph, in her elusiveness, remains at the periphery of Cyclopean vision despite the giant's obsession with her, somewhat like a flickering light glimpsed at the very edge of vision. She resembles Stevens' "Angel of Reality," an apparition never wholly grasped by the eye:

> Am I not,
> Myself, only half of a figure of a sort,
>
> A figure half seen, or seen for a moment, a man
> Of the mind, an apparition apparelled in
>
> Apparels of such lightest look that a turn
> Of my shoulder and quickly, too quickly, I am gone?
> (*CP* 497)

Góngora's vision of the goddess in flight is the imperfectly glimpsed reality which eludes, as "apparition," its too-avid suitor. The much sought-after goddess of Sicily, a "goddess of reality," appears and disappears, always outpacing her pursuers:

> Cuál diente mortal, cuál metal fino
> la fuga suspender podría ligera
> que el desdén solicita?
> (133-135)

The "diente mortal" is the fatal sting of the asp or serpent which strikes Eurydice as she flees, and the "metal fino" is the gold of the apples which distract Atalanta. Galatea as *dea abscondita* is perceived by her unsuccessful suitors as perennially mobile and barely visible, "A figure half seen, or seen for a moment." Only Acis knows how to wait, to be silently and patiently attentive. As the goddess who presides over the fruitfulness of Sicily, its harvest of wheat and grapes, Galatea, like Venus, signifies *physis* and becoming. But she is also equivalent to *physis* in its residue of hiddenness, for she personifies all that eludes the seizure of Saturnine conceptualization. If Polyphemus is dedicated to the boundaries which support his inflated identity, and to including more and more of the world within those boundaries, Galatea in turn effaces the very boundaries upon which the ego insists. She is a reality which shakes free of appropriations.

Amphibious creatures have long attracted the attention of thinkers, perhaps because they seem to point a fundamental attribute of mental activity itself – the sensation well known to thinkers of the failure of conceptualization in the face of an ever-receding, flickering reality which defies classification, and the puzzlement and sense of loss which may follow upon this ill-fated task. Even Aristotle was apparently bemused by these marginal regions, which in fact supported his vision of nature as a continuum. He was moved to acknowledge the occasional resistance of natural phenomena to classification when he observed beings which seemed to occupy two categories – bats (earth and air), seals (land and water), and sponges (neither animal nor vegetable). (Lovejoy 56)[7]

In the seventeenth century scientists, like the physicists of our own era, delighted openly in the enigmatic and paradoxical; their field of vision and observation was a universe of conceits, a droll and artful discourse which provided archetypes of wit for the poet and rhetorician. Francis Bacon confesses his bewilderment and wonder at the "singular instances" among natural phenomena, those beings which seem miraculous by virtue of their suspension between two conditions or categories of being, citing as examples moss, comets, flying fishes and bats. (Scoular 33-34) To the Italian

---

[7] Aristotle's acceptance of the limits of classification suggests to Lovejoy two contrasting styles of thinking: "... there are not many differences in mental habit more significant than that of thinking in discrete, well-defined concepts and that of thinking in terms of continuity, of infinitely delicate shadings-off of everything into something else, of the overlapping of essences, so that the whole notion of species comes to seem an artifice of thought not truly applicable to the fluency, the, so to say, over-lappingness of the real world." (57)

rhetorician Tesauro, such ambivalent creatures are *argutezza della natura*, evidence of God's wit: satyrs, the minotaur, sea-oxen, the phoenix, silkworm and tortoise all belong in this collection of *mirabili*. (Scoular 30) These elusive creatures are biological flourishes whose ambiguity speaks to the protean flux of the universe and invites contemplation of divine caprice. They ornament the book of nature and provide aesthetic delight for the student of *physis*.

Like other amphibian creatures, Galatea is always poised for departure, moving from sea to land and back to sea again, carried on the wings of an immortal disdain. Instead of climbing up or sinking down, she circulates, and in this characteristic movement she resembles the element of water itself. She personifies, in addition, the gesture of recoil, just as her giant suitor is fixed in the posture of mania for possession. She attracts desire, and moves way from it. The imploring Glaucus is hoarse from pleading with her to join him on the "silver fields" of the waves (117-120), and the Cyclops' song, conversely, urges her to abandon the sea for his earthly domain. The perpetual flight generated by her disdain for her suitors is the most obvious cause of her mobility, and yet her circulation between land and sea places her beyond the immediate context of mere alarm at unsought attentions.

Galatea's identity, as well as her divinity, is fluid, and as Walter Pabst points out she is yet another of Góngora's personifications of the sea, which for Góngora is a living and sublime being, a symbol of perpetual creation. (83-84) But perhaps more significantly, the characteristically elusive movement of the nymph reminds us of the circulation of *physis*, its circuit of revealing and concealing which places it beyond the grasp of conceptual formulation, of metaphysics. The circulation of the goddess is an inhuman event which refers only to itself. The gracefulness and beauty of the poet's description of Galatea in Stanza 13 testifies to the fact that Galatea is less human than her monstrous admirer. For we are given a description of a girl which never quite coheres; we see not the girl, but a *candida diva* in her abstracted qualities, as though they floated somewhere above her: whiteness, feathers, stars, crystal. The eye stops at the surface; there is no contour or bulk indicative of a corporal being. It is not a specific girl that Góngora conjures up but an idea of divine feminine beauty, a "summing up" or unfolding of the three Graces of Venus: "Galatea es su nombre, y dulce en ella / el terno Venus de sus gracias suma." (99-100)

In Stanza 20 the poet, having identified the nymph as the island's deity, "bien sea religión, bien amor sea, / deidad, aunque sin templo, es Galatea," (151-52) elaborates her divinity into the locale of its worship by the islanders:

> Sin aras no: que el margen donde para
> del espumoso mar su pie ligero
> al labrador, de sus primicias ara,
> de sus esquilmos es al ganadero;
> de la Copia – a la tierra, poco avara –
> el cuerno vierte el hortelano, entero,
> sobre la mimbre que tejió, prolija,
> si artificiosa no, su honesta hija.

> [Shrineless, but yet she has an altar where
> Her light step pauses by the foaming sea,
> On which both herd and ploughman offer her
> The tithes and first fruits of their industry;
> Grudged nothing by the soil, the gardener
> Empties his horn of plenty liberally
> Into the osier which, though ill designed,
> With no small toil his worthy daughter twined.]

Galatea's altar, like the nymph herself, is mobile; its site is acknowledged by her worshippers to be wherever her foot happens to touch down on sand when she emerges from the foamy sea.

It is crucial to place Góngora's interest in boundary locales, sites where different elements or geographies intersect, in the context of the Venusian atmosphere of the poem. Such sites represent another dimension of an aesthetic which tends to favor images of origin, of conditions in which life emerges. This habit of mind reconstructs in the highly sophisticated an stylized terms of *culteranismo* a feature of primitive imagination which locates generation in places where two or more elements can be seen to fuse – as in storm clouds, or on the surface of the sea, especially close to the shore.[8] This fascination with the marginal places of

---

[8] Jack Yeats claimed, speaking of the role of northwestern Ireland in the formation of his brother's imagination, that there was an ancient belief that where fresh water rushes into the sea in the form of a short river (he was thinking of the Garavoque, which links Lough Gill to Sligo Bay) "a kind of magic is generated and spread upon the whole neighborhood." (Henn 16)

generation, a dominant feature of Góngora's imagination, informs his depiction of the Venusian nymph. It also explains a motive in the Cyclops' attraction to her. He would like to possess the more numinous life she seems to represent, by removing her from the "reino de la espuma" and making her a part of his own inclusive landscape, by removing her from the disturbingly boundless to the bounded and circumscribed. He yearns to possess the life which eludes his grasp, except in the form of ownership: his prized herd of goats, beehives and vineyards, the human heads which adorned the wall of his cave before love inclined him to more hospitable manners. His fantasy of her pearl-generating feet (Ovid's Polyphemus merely begs Galatea to show her head from beneath the blue waves, XXII 838-39) echoes the poet's own vision of Galatea's altar, conjuring the boundary space between sea and land where magic may be generated.[8] In ancient Greece the deity most often identified with the generation of life is Aphrodite, whose origin is reflected in her other name, Anadyomene, or "goddess rising from the sea." Her first representation in sculpture is by Pheidias, (5th c.), who places her with one foot raised and resting on a tortoise – a creature connected with the goddess as an agent of creation. (Suhr 50) Like Venus, the tortoise is a marginal or liminal phenomenon, not contained wholly by either of two territories, removed, one might say, from the fixedness of the *caverna profunda* which is the antithesis to the light and mobility of the goddess. While Polyphemus sets boundaries to his territory, placing himself at the center, Galatea transgresses these boundaries, ubiquitous and mobile like light or water.

Polyphemus does nonetheless trace a kind of psychic movement, an emergence from inner pain to explication and finally violent discharge of that pain. The Cyclops, like Vulcan, was a type of artisan in ancient literature and mythology, but when he moves from metalworking to poetry his art becomes for the first time, not only a bridge from inner pain to objective beauty, but the first evidence of his interior life. The myth of the Cyclops acquires pathos; the ugliness and monstrosity of the creature of epic and legend takes on a psychology of inner suffering. Where in Homer his suffering was a result of physical maiming, his characterization has now surpassed that of Vulcan, the maimed artisan, because his deformity is now internal. (Vulcan's cuckolding does not interfere with his work, as we see in the *Odyssey* VIII, but rather incites to higher levels of artistry.)

This pathos in turn moves into association with the realm of illusion, fantasy, even mirage. In an essay on the psychology of aesthetics Hanna Segal observes that the "ugly" is present in all the major aesthetic categories – tragic, comic, realistic, – except one: classical beauty. But the sublimations of the work of classical beauty, while they ostensibly exclude the ugly, the monstrous and the deformed, in fact embody a "deep experience," that is, a deep depression, which overcomes itself only in a perfect and integrated beauty. (206) Wilhelm Worringer's idea of "self-alienation" in aesthetic experience has a similar relevance to the Cyclops of pastoral song. Style itself, according to Worringer's idea of the "will to form," is a means of "emancipation" from contingency and temporality. (8,44) In its most abstract or idealized manifestations, artistic form serves to conceal depth. It is a refuge from the abysmal self. Góngora's poem includes both the representation of the monstrous, which, as Segal comments, "expresses the state of the internal world in depression" and which "includes tension, hatred, and its results – the destruction of good and whole objects . . ." (206) and the classical beauty which represents a sublimation of "the world in depression" which is the monstrous.

The "will to form" is the active imagination pressing back against what Stevens calls the "pressure of reality," and a kind of "violence" in itself. (*The Necessary Angel* 36) The Cyclopean eruption into song is both an expression of the giant's bondage to desire and of the "ecstatic freedom of the mind" (35) which is the privilege of the poet. His song springs from the need to find relief from the contingency of the world and the depth of the self. In Stanza 13 the giant is submerged and "lost" in aesthetic contemplation – intention and desire have become momentarily eclipsed. But this moment of absorption in the thing desired is depicted by the author, and not by his creature, whose own song retains the *dolor interno*, the pain of the inner self upon which pure aesthetic experience stumbles.

Of the many sea-deities mentioned in Góngora's poem, it is the Venusian Galatea who is able to transcend her element and to carry over the creative principle of the sea onto land. She makes the evolutionary leap, but reserves the right to circulate. The sea, personified in these various divinities – Neptune, Thetis, Glaucus,

Palaemon – is one of the two elemental regions, sea and light, which constitute the lemental framework of his fiction, although they do not always remain in the background. Of the therapeutic properties of light and water and their affinity with the human eye, Ficino writes in *De vita triplici* (62):

> ... sight is a ray that is naturally lifted up by a certain water in our eyes, and it seeks a tempered light in the water, a light that to a certain extent resists it. Thus water delights us, and we take pleasure in mirrors, and enjoy anything green.

In Góngora's poem the *aphros* of aesthetic experience is a fantasy of release from time, equivalent to Ficino's idea that Venus provides a release from the grip of Saturn. In this "will to form" the depth of Chronos/Kronos reaches outwards towards the horizontal expanse which is the realm of the aesthetic, and ultimately to that point in the spectrum where, as in H. D.'s poem "Tribute to the Angels" (XLIII), "all lights become one."[9] The release into whiteness signifies not only the repose of desire, the cessation of willing, but the arrival at the point of beginning again. This whiteness of perennial departure is suggested by the whiteness of the dawn goddess, ancestor to Aphrodite, who drives away her sister Night in the Hymn to Dawn in the *Rig-Veda* (I.113): "And she shall shine out in all the days to come. Undecaying, undying, she moves with her own laws." (Friederich 194)

It is worth noting that while the "reino de la espuma" signifies for Góngora the place of aesthetic experience, this realm is organic, a flowering of *physis* suffused with and shaped by human intention. The aesthetic in Góngora is not therefore essentially

---

[9] And the point in the spectrum
where all the lights become one,

is white and white is not no-colour,
as we were told as children,

but all colour;
where the flames mingle

and the wings meet, where we gain
the arc of perfection.

We are satisfied, we are happy,
we being again;

(*Trilogy* 109)

other than the organic, nor is it imposed on the organic, but originates at the point at which organic phenomena become gratuitous appearance, appearing for the sake of appearance, display, ostentation – to give pleasure to the eye and mind. In his vision of Galatea and her realm of sea-spume the poet has brought to full realization an idea of the sea as a vast depth perennially moving towards its consummation, in union with air and sunlight, in the form of *aphros* and Venus.

CHAPTER IV

CONCLUSION

> "What you see from the top of the cliff, in sweetness, is the first-born being arising out of the waters, Aphrodite, who has been born in the swirl of liquid spirals, Nature being born in smiling voluptuousness."
>
> Michel Serres, Hermes

1. POLARITIES: A RECAPITULATION

Let us return briefly to the idea of Venus underlying Góngora's poetics in the *Polifemo* before taking up the problem of Polyphemus and his difficult relation to language and poetry. Of the many types of Venus found in Classical literature it is the Epicurean Venus which Góngora's goddess most evokes. The Lucretian Venus breaks free of Olympus to become for the Epicurean poet the symbol of his physics, a system of thought which attempts to come to terms with the havoc and randomness of the natural world. According to Lucretian materialism, all natural forms arise form the random combinations of atoms which ceaselessly fall, swerve, and combine, and it is Venus who mediates the chaos of origin and the configurations which emerge from the random play of particles of matter. She appears in the poem's invocation as the principle of creation in the universe and as the power the poet calls upon to sponsor his enterprise, as she does all creative endeavor:

> Though you all living creatures are conceived and come forth to look upon the sunlight. Before you the winds flee, and at

your coming the clouds forsake the sky. For you the inventive earth flings up sweet flowers.... Since you alone are the guiding power of the universe and without you nothing emerges into the sunlit world to grow in joy and loveliness, yours is the partnership I seek in striving to compose these lines... (27)

In this manifesto of naturalism, Venus is *natura naturans*, the spirit of matter and of the ceaseless transformations of phenomena. She is not only mediatrix between chaos and form, but the irrational impulse behind the *swerving* of atoms, and so personifies the inextricable linkage between creation and destruction, as well as the incurable dividedness of the human soul. And so among the effects of Venusian presence Lucretius includes disorder, pain, anguish, war. Venus will not relinquish Mars.

The erotic disorder which afflicts the pastoral world in Stanzas 21 and 22 of Góngora's poem, beginning with "arde la juventud," "youth is on fire," recall the Lucretian vision of a universe subject to Venusian swervings: straying livestock and torrents of melting snow, the breaking up of the stasis of winter, the dislocations of passion. While Saturn evokes a violence of darkness and captivity beneath the earth, the emergence of the year into light is violent in its own way; it moves us into the always hazardous realm of possibility: the ploughman's oxen stray, *errantes* like their master, the shepherd wanders, the wolf stalks his prey in daylight. (St. 22)[1] As he prepares the cool bower where Acis and Galatea meet, the poet calls on *Amor* to call back ("revoca") the shepherd's whistle and wake the sheepdog, while fully recognizing that the blood-stained grass complements the altar on the beach, the prodigious fertility of the orchards, vineyards and wheatfields ripening in the heat and volcanic soil of Sicily. Wandering and straying into danger is a condition of plenitude, burgeoning growth, the emer-

---

[1] Michel Serres writes of the Lucretian Venus: "Venus assembles the atoms, like the compounds. She is not transcendent like the other gods, but immanent in this world, the being of relation. She is identical to the relation. *Venus sive natura sive coniuncta foedera*. She inspires inclination; she *is* inclination." (114) Inclination, swerving, *declinando* (Gr. *clinamen*) is the principle in Lucretian physics which allows for natural forms to arise from the random combinations of atoms, which fall, swerve, collide and combine. See also Kenneth Burke, *A Grammar of Motives*, 160.

gence of new forms into the world. A voluptuous space is engendered in profound disequilibrium, a fruitful turbulence.

Against this turbulent space of creation the giant goatherd looms as a massively dissident figure, just as devouring Saturn and those solitary brooders held in his thrall dissent from the web of relations which is the province of Venus. The discordancy of Saturn and Venus accounts for the main tensions of the poem and gives shape to its meditation on the abysmally human and its difficult relations with the perennial and evanescent "beginning again" of creation. We can see, schematized in the following set of contrasting values, that each divinity lays claim to the whole of reality; each is a perspective and a center of meaning:

Saturn	*Venus*
Time-depth	Space-surface
Subjectivism	Objectivism
Monstrosity	Beauty
Language	Silence
Darkness	Light, whiteness, color

Each column of words assigns to the other an ephemeral existence: for the human depth of Saturn the beauty of Aphrodite is a cruel mirage over which language haplessly casts its net, and which time effaces; the realm of Venus is a hallucinatory object to the depth of subjectivity, its will and its desire. It lacks density and weight and may vanish, and yet, paradoxically, it comprises an apparition which may shatter the density of the fixed self, like the lure of imagination, fantasy, and aesthetics. And in the realm of beauty monstrosity is deviant, accidental, formally incomplete, doomed to concealment and blindness, the ultimate deprivation, of light itself.

Two modes of being: existence as privation (the subjective mode), and existence as plenitude and a flowering of consummate form (the mode of *aphros*). Time and depth and inwardness constitute the mode of human subjectivism – the blind promontory of the Cyclopean gaze and thundering voice. Language arises in the cleft between the two modes. As lyric, measured utterance it retains the clamor of the cry as it moves towards the Venusian realm, the "reino de la espuma." The act of self-overcoming which is a motive of aesthetic language, the break with the titanic and monstrous reality of an anguished world on the margin of form, is never fully achieved in the "fiercer song" of the Cyclops. The song cannot be fully realized in the manner of a painting or a work of architecture because of the persistent drift back towards the inarticulate, the inner dolor.

2. CYCLOPEAN LANGUAGE

Rilke, writing of Rodin, remarks on the closure and self-containment of the plastic arts, making an implicit comparison with verbal discourse:

> However great the movement in a piece of sculpture, whether it comes from infinite distances or from the depths of the heavens, it must return to the marble, the vast circle must be closed, that circle of solitude within which a work of art exists. . . . This distinguishing characteristic of things, complete self-absorption, was what gave to plastic art its calm; it must have neither desire nor expectation beyond itself, nor bear any reference to what lies beyond, nor be aware of anything outside itself. Its surroundings must be found within it. (107)

Unlike sculpture or painting, verbal language not only moves beyond itself, but it seeks and fails to achieve the circle of containment in fusion with its object; it remains stretched between the silence of its object and its own originating darkness and silence, the darkness and silence in human consciousness. In its irrevocable contract with human expectation, it is neither wholly self-absorbed nor consumed in that contract with the reality which always lies beyond it, and which is, like Stevens' "angel of reality," "half seen, or seen for a moment," then gone.

We cannot fail to note amongst the neat oppositions cited above a certain incongruity in the placement of language in the column which includes darkness and monstrosity. For language surely brings to light and makes intelligible, in lyric poetry, what would otherwise be the incoherence of human emotion, and so belongs to the realm of Venus and *physis*, moving towards *aphros*, consciousness and disclosure. And yet it adheres to the dark side of the *discordia concors* of Venus and Mars; it is a colossal disturbance, like a bolt of lightning, an earthquake, a volcanic eruption, the crushing boulder falling on the bower and on the fleeing Acis. Language is the eruption of human presence, as mutation, in the universe. Cyclopean language is founded upon the monster's condition of being a disruption in the world, vortex, a fathomless cave of devouring energy, a Hades. It is the language of that species identified by Nietzsche as "das noch nicht fest gestellte Tier," the animal whose type is not yet determined or fixed. Cyclopean song reminds us that language does not appear in the world of forms. Its relation to other forms is compromised by its forlorn, strident and menacing courtship of its object.

While Cyclopean language carries the human voice beyond the immediacy of the animal cry to a kind of lyrical promontory and aspires to the status of inscription (in St. 52 the sky itself becomes like the vault of the cave, etched with a history of amorous suffering), it carries with it distortion and negation. It brings the gravity and chaos of the cave into the world in the form of the misperceptions of the encaved and armored self, and so makes a vortex in the field of Being. Cyclopean language also construes a tower — an eyeless lighthouse, and a self-consuming light. The doomed courtship which is Cyclopean language links up momentarily the incoherence of a feeling and suffering self to the world it inhabits and imagines, and then collapses, a broken bridge, pulled down by the gravity of its rootedness in subjectivity.

Yet how can Polyphemus be both a vestige of primeval underworld powers and a symbol of human consciousness? Saturn, as we have seen, is among other things the name for the force which withdraws us from the visible world. Language mitigates this withdrawal, mediating between the hiddenness of Saturn and the open space of the world. Consciousness, in the cycle of Saturn and Venus, withdraws from and returns to the world, and the return of consciousness to visibility and to relation is marked by dissonance, a reverberation of distress. The Cyclops, in his periodic seclusion within the sealed cave, and in the helplessness of his melancholy, is a figure for the troublesome interiority of human consciousness and its place in the world of visible form.[2] His

---

[2] "Seen from the perspective of the world of appearances and the activities conditioned by it, the main characteristic of mental activities is their *invisibility*." (Arendt 71) Arendt goes on to distinguish between mind (active) and soul (passive), which compete for rule over interior life.

ascent from cavern to cliff is the primordial event of language, in which the sealed mouth of the cave becomes the mouth of lyric utterance in a shocked universe:

> Cuando, de amor el fiero jayán ciego,
> la cerviz oprimió a una roca brava
> que a la playa, de escollos no desnuda,
> linterna es ciega y atalaya muda.
>
> (341-44)

> [Blinded by love, the savage giant came
> His ponderous foot upon a cliff to lay
> Which, soaring high, surveyed the rock-strewn coast,
> An eyeless light, a silent sentry-post.]

The cavern has undergone a metamorphosis: its inwardness becomes a bellowing mouth which activates the barbarous pipes, and then becomes the impulse for Cyclopean song itself, which roars and reverberates in the numerous sea grottoes of western Sicily. Ingestion, the blind swallowing of the world, is succeeded by breathing, which feeds the bellows of the pipes and makes the breather of these colossal sounds an "arbiter" of mountains and seashore. (345)

From the discordant meeting of self and world, and the alternately dismayed and arrogant recognition of the boundaries between the two, arises the figure of the ego, which wills its *arbitration*, its rearrangements of the landscape. Before the act of song, the giant announces his presence to the world. His posture is a "standing before" the world, and the world "is brought to stand and into position." (Heidegger, *Poetry* 110) As a promontory which oversees the placid ocean (a sapphire mirror) the classical Cyclops assumes his modern identity: man the arbiter, who recasts other beings into an "objective inventory," "given over to, commended to and thus subjected to the command of self-assertive production." (111) This baroque formulation of the Cyclops is nothing less than the emergence of Heidegger's technological man, to whom the world, and ultimately himself, is raw material.

His second act, fatally entangled in the first, is an act of imagination: the absent Galatea, never actually seen, is summoned into presence, and with her, an entire kingdom of ultimate meaning, a place of radiance and bliss which will put an end to suffering and history. But the production of images which follows upon the initial exclamation, like the primary act of self-assertion and positioning, does not detach itself from the original *caverna*, but carries the human darkness over into the world, casting into play a chiaroscuro pattern of depth and lighted presence. The song, a plaintive apostrophe, re-calls what is no longer present to vision, and wills its return ("deja las ondas," "Pisa la arena,") in the form of a complex of associated images which constitute the "reino de la espuma."

3. POETRY AND MEDIATION

Góngora was at one time called, disparagingly, "príncipe de las tinieblas," or "prince of shadows," an epithet meant to equate "darkness" with the difficulty posed by the dense, tangled texture of his verse. And, in fact, he may be the first Spanish poet of an evocative darkness and absence: in the early stanzas of the *Polifemo*, he assembles his materials of negativity – bones, ashes, darkness, heavy sleep, the cries of nocturnal birds – attributes of primal night and earth. These materials compose a monstrous habitat, but they also connote the tomb of words, the place where language is eclipsed by the absolute, hidden self in the utter barrenness of deep melancholy. For melancholy is by its nature inimical to language, since the inwardness and withdrawal it induces extends beyond the inwardness of thinking, feeling consciousness. It represents the crisis of language in paralysis, the end-point of introversion.

Walter Benjamin cites, in his exploration of melancholy and its relation to baroque allegory, the "enormous, anti-artistic subjectivity of the Baroque." (233) The allegories of the Baroque, he maintains, are products of the forge of subjectivity, like gems formed by the earth's concentrated density. Benjamin's reading of the German Baroque leans towards the Cyclopean, concentrating on the dark side of the baroque duality, of the *chiaroscuro* of radical subjectivism and its formal denial. But it is the overcoming of radical subjectivism which concerns Góngora, who constructs his "rimas sonoras" by wedding this subjectivity – his own subjectivity concealed behind the mask of the Cyclops – to crystal, stars, lilies, pearls, and the swan's white plumage; to the whiteness of *aphros* which is the white robe of the dancing sage, redeemed from his bitter sagacity by art, by immersion in aesthetic experience.

The act of self-overcoming and sublimation in aesthetic experience can be figured in the separation of a specific figure from its ground: Galatea, for example, is a "scythe" in Stanza 28, who by the act of rising to a standing position severs her own whiteness from the grass: ". . . a los verdes márgenes ingrata, / segur se hizo de sus azucenas" (220) (Ungrateful to the green banks, she made herself a scythe to her own lilies). The poet's artifice, like the nymph's rising from the grass, may seem to turn away from nature with disdain and ingratitude. But the fierce negation of nineteenth century dandyism is missing. Galatea may be said to enact her own coming into being from the background of nature which is her source. She makes a timeless image of beginning: a primordial efflorescence from the green sea of her generation. In her, as in Stevens' "angel of earth," we see the earth again, without its heaviness. The poet's diamond-like inscriptions rise, in the same way, as a radically individualized and stylized distillation of the anonymous "inner dolor," the universal human background: the grass of human origin, wandering and end.[3]

Góngora uses the scythe image twice: the second scything image occurs as a forecast of Acis' fate, which the narrator inserts before presenting the Cyclops' song. The nymph, hearing the savage sound of the pipes, lies trembling in the arms of her lover, to whom she clings as vine to elm: ". . . infelice olmo que pedazos / la segur de los celos hará aguda". (355-56) Acis, the narrator tells us, is an unhappy elm who will be hacked apart by the sharp scythe of the monster's jealousy. This scythe of jealousy, by means of which the poem leaps ahead momentarily to its denouement, is also the scythe of Kronos/Chronos; the Saturnine instrument of time and death and the disappearance of all things from the visible

---

[3] James Hillman, in "Silver and the White Earth" I.21-47, writes that in ancient metallurgy the "release of the white dove" meant the separation of silver from the heavier lead with which it was bound in the earth. We are also meant to understand this metaphor in the psychological sense of a release from the literal into a metaphorical and poetic consciousness. But Hillman reminds us that melancholy follows upon this release: "the more white reflection the more burdened lead; as we produce the silver, we increase the lead." He equates the depression of the thinker with the mine – it cannot be done away with, for it is the substance from which we extract the precious metal.

world. It serves the law of finitude, the boundary imposed by the setting sun, or the transit of the comet to which the Cyclops is compared. The scythe of lilies is the scythe of artistic creation which severs the imagination from the *fiero canto* of will and desire, and allows us to see the world anew.

Insofar as Góngora can be shown to explore the interrelations of language, light and darkness, and insofar as he acknowledges, like his contemporary Caravaggio, that darkness as well as light is the place of poetic language, Góngora earns the title "prince of shadows."[4] Heidegger remarks of the "saying" of images in poetry that it "gathers the brightness and sound of the heavenly appearances into one with the darkness and silence of what is alien." (*Poetry* 226) The enterprise of poetic language is always a study of *chiaroscuro;* the darkness seeking out, menacing and clasping to it the crystallization of a remote galactic whiteness and silence. Like the image of the estuary in Góngora's *Soledad segunda*, avid to consume and to be consumed by, as "cristalina mariposa," the salt crystal of the ocean, language is always moving toward its own annihilation, and yet its trajectory is never complete, its darkness never annihilated in light.

It is the human "saying" of images which makes a bridge between these areas of silence, which are the inhuman boundaries of human consciousness.[5] The silence of darkness and the silence of light await the animating bridge of poetry. We return to the original link between monstrosity and darkness: in the context of the two regions of utter darkness and utter light, the Cyclops

---

[4] The "prince of shadows" epithet assigned Góngora is also his Cyclopean mask in this poem, understood as the inverse of Yeats' idea of mask: instead of the mask as a sublimation of the private and sentimental into the active and formal, Góngora's mask is a symbol of inwardness, desire, violence – anti-poetry. It presents the poet in disguise, a monstrous embodiment of his vulnerability as an artist.

[5] Charles Scott, in *Boundaries in Mind*, writes of the regions of "utter darkness and utter light" which form these boundaries: "Utter darkness may be thought of as imprisonment. But it may also be found as the backdrop of an obscure freedom, wild and primordial, foreign to us, yet vaguely compelling. And the freedom of pure light may threaten a freedom and madness no less than darkness without light. Both 'elements' have been narrated in early Greek mythology, and that mythology may be taken as chronicling regions of being. Their genealogy and ways of happening speak of how non-objective and non-particular alertness occurs, of the immediacy of mind un-circumscribed by any domain of identity." (109)

marks the point where absolute darkness is compromised by an anguished stirring, by the sounds of an emerging human existence. This pre-existence, evolving from its chaos, passes through a threshold and arrives at a primitive, deficient form: monstrosity, and the void and density of the Cyclops' origin becomes compromised by an engagement with the structures of the daylit world.

The saying of images brings to bear, in a situation of pronounced estrangement, the possibility of an attentiveness to things, and also the possibility of relationship and accord. For Polyphemus reaches not only towards possession, but conjunction, the Venusian contract, the completed identity. So while we recognize that the kinship of language and monstrosity is fundamental, we acknowledge too the volatility of language, its capacity to make incursions into the "flowering season" of Being, the *estación florida*.[6] Its territory is always the uncertain space between the concealment of the cave and the full display of the unrepentant peacock.

As we have seen, Cyclopean song, which is the "fiero canto" of the poet, is too fragile to sustain itself as a bridge to *aphros* and the irradiating power which the Cyclops fails to bring to earth — that is, to his own inner "earth." It quickly deteriorates into angry shouts when the shepherd sees the "sacrilegious" goats trampling the tender grape vines. He shifts quickly to a concern with his possessions — with the *negotium* which is never remote from his consciousness; his wrath flares up and he regresses to his Homeric, stone-hurling self. The shift in his attention from his fantasy of Galatea as Venus (a Venus on the sea, soon to become a "Cupid on the mountains" when she has accepted his gift of bow and quiver) to the goats and violated plants marks an abrupt descent into the heaviness which has been associated with the giant throughout the poem. The precarious span of his song, which has carried him into unfamiliar regions, has been haunted throughout by the force of gravity: the gravity of the cave, its circling wreath of birds whose motion mocks the buoyancy of flight, the rough stone portal, the "grave peso" of the shepherd's tree-like staff, the solidity of light itself, which the giant treads upon in Stanza 9: "pisando la dudosa luz del día" (72) as he drives his oxen home at

---

[6] See Góngora's *Soledad primera:* "Era del año la estación florida." I take the season represented by these first lines to be a powerful and concentrated statement of Góngora's poetics, his aesthetics of efflorescence.

CONCLUSION 117

the end of the day. Gravity of sound, light, and space; and gravity of the would-be bridegroom who boasts in Stanza 51 of being "tanto esposo" – "so much bridegroom": never has the sun, in its passage from the frozen north to the extreme heat of the Indies (406-08) seen such a sheer quantity of bridegroom.

The giant's excursion into lyricism breaks off with his projected song's displacement by a literal projectile, the stone missile, and falls back into its originating heaviness. With "infinite" violence he wrenches off a jagged piece of the rocky cliff: "con violencia desgajó infinita, / la mayor punta de la excelsa roca,". The *dolor interno*, the poet tells us, remains; it is like the reverberation of a bass note *sostenuto*, a *basso profundo* above which an ephemeral play of harmonies has vanished.[7] It is the beating heart, this dolorous bass note, of the entire enclosing narration which continues after the Cyclops' voice is silenced.

His song is a bridge which dissolves, a *musical* phenomenon which passes, but which is enclosed by the space of the poem, *verba* enclosed by *scripta*, (while beyond the script, the poem, is the *pasando* of the poet himself.) It is the style of the poet which makes a bridge between the lower and upper realms of "pure" depth and "pure" surface, between darkness and light. Style steps across the abyss; it reunites the dislocated in a heterodox universe of its own devising.

If we recall that the giant begins his song as the sun is setting, and that Polyphemus imagines his eye to rival Helios (421), then we can see that his song traces the last phase of the diurnal cycle of the sun as we perceive it. The flash of lightning too, another form of Cyclopean light, makes its violent appearance and is gone. That the Cyclops longs for a different order of light is evident in Stanza 47, when he asks the nymph to leave the ocean so that her feet may bestow their magic silver on the shells of the beach. (374-376) The descend of the chariot of Helios that brings in its wake the dark (371) yields place to an aesthetic light – the same silver light

---

[7] The sustained, brooding power of the *basso sostenuto* provides the "gravity" of sonatas from Gabrielli (d. 1612) to Corelli (d. 1713). In baroque monody the distribution of sound is essentially different from that of Renaissance polyphony, in which the various parts of a vocal composition, for example, carry equal weight. The entire harmony of a baroque sonata was constructed on a *basso continuo*, a continuous bass played on a keyboard instrument in unison with a bass melody instrument.

that overtakes the broken world as the fable moves into metamorphosis.

The period of the day is the pastoral unit of time; but here the poet focuses on the second half of the day's cycle, between the fullness of noon and the sinking light of evening. In the "full noon" passage, the Cyclops seems most fully real to himself: space seems to converge upon this point, upon the solar eye and its dazzling reflection in the compliant water. The time of the song is the time of this illusion: the sunlight is poised to disappear at the time that the song breaks off and the Cyclops' attention is diverted from his fantasy. The advent of evening is the moment when the seemingly solid – "tanta vista," "tanto esposo," dissolves.

In the decline of sunlight and of Cyclopean song, we have an image of history itself, declining towards its night as the gods flee. (Heidegger, *Poetry* 81) The vanishing sunlight, together with the appearance of the silver water, suggests an alchemy whose last phases have been reversed, since it fashions silver from the heat of gold. With the conversion of Acis' blood to "cristal" (496) and then "líquido aljófar" (liquid pearl), and his bones to "corriente plata" (flowing silver) language moves from Cyclopean light into Venusian waters. The mediation is complete, and the poet has worked through his *fiero canto* and proceeds to enclose it, transforming the comet-like light of its human fire into the silver light of the river, a new image of temporality: flux and metamorphosis rather than the solar rise and decline which resembles the ego's alternating postures of confident self-affirmation and melancholy withdrawal or recession. The quicksilver of metamorphosis releases matter from the weight of the Saturnine, its fatal gravity. The process is both poesis and therapy, a means of healing which employs the language of *aesthesis*, as distinguished from the language of will and desire.

The concealment of the cave and the appetite of its monstrous inhabitant are the hidden side of the poet, his dark twin, anti-poetry – Orpheus' shadow-self. Beings – deer, stones, trees – fell into a pattern, arranging themselves around the central magnetic sound of the Orphic lyre and voice. Music, in the story of Orpheus, instigated a second ordering of Creation, a concord which is inverted by the anti-orphism of Polyphemus' bellowing pipes and roaring voice. The Cyclops is the threat that non-being, concealed in the earth's depths, poses to the upper world; Ovid figures this recurrent threat in Hades' excursion to the earth's surface where, lured by Venus, he discovers and rapes Persephone. Hades is the shadow of poesis, and lies within the poet himself. It is his innermost life and the ever-present possibility of his failure as an artist, the failure of language to reconstruct the world from inner chaos. Góngora projects this sense of failure into the Cyclops, who, as the shadow-self, fails to achieve the unity he seeks, the light restored by the eyes of Galatea.

The Cyclops remains a symbol of desire and longing throughout the poem; the inner Cyclops *is* pure longing, while the "outer" Cyclops, the Cyclops-proprietor, is a fixed being who in turn fixes and encloses. Thus his world is split into two areas or dimensions: the territory he possesses and controls: the *actuality*, the fulfilled world of harvest and still-life – the "become;" and the intangible, inaccessible world in space, the world *to which he has not yet come*, a bright, always-receding horizon. As Spengler remarks of the "Faustian" world, as opposed to the world of classical pastoral, we may also observe of the Cyclopean mode of awareness: it is the deepened, temporal world of yearning, as opposed to the pastoral continuous present; it is Eve's awakening, in Calderón's *auto*, from the flowery meadows of the *candor primero* to the anguished time of her inner life.

Góngora's poem explores the relations between two kinds of illumination in such a way that the poet seems to comment on the doomed, comet-like trajectory of the human will from the perspective of his own failed worldly life.[8] The court position fails to materialize, patrons vanish, the nymph recedes further into limitless marine space. Polyphemus loses control of the poem and resumes his identity of maimed, Homeric ogre. And the poet whose muse is the "culta sí, aunque bucólica" Thalia, the comic muse, now comes to the foreground. The silver, mediating light of metamorphosis is neither darkness nor light, which resist human meaning, but a light which arises from aesthetic activity, and the bridging of both utterly inhuman realms: poesis.

---

[8] John Beverley calls attention to the image of the marble castle that appears near the end of the *Soledad segunda*. The castle, of white Parian marble, stands on a cliff above the sea, and its silver capitals reflect the light of the setting sun so precisely that the pilgrim, approaching from the sea, can count each ray. Unlike the silver water of the *Polifemo*, here silver is joined to the monumental whiteness of the building, which "conveys a feeling of the eternal and the absolute: a monument closed against time..." (108)

4. The Heraldry of the Imagination

In Wallace Stevens' "The Idea of Order at Key West" a singing girl is posed against the sea. The sky grows dark. The sea makes its inhuman sounds, and the girl makes a world with her song:

> And when she sang,
> the sea,
> whatever self it had, became the self that was her song
> for she was the maker. Then we,
> as we beheld her striding there alone,
> knew that there never was a world for her
> except the one she sang, and singing, made.
> (CP 129-130)

The sea is "ever-hooded, tragic-gestured," repeating its "meaningless plungings." The girl is "the single artificer of the world in which she sang."[9] When the singing ends the speaker turns towards the town, and the lights of the fishing boats harbored there seem to master the vast expanse of night and sea, arranging its depths into measured zones. The lights, like the singing voice, speak the "Blessed rage for order" which seeks both mastery of self and of the ground and origin of self. The girl stands at the boundary between world and sea, standing there in order to make the song. The figure of the girl, her voice that "made / the sky acutest at its vanishing" and the "glassy lights" of the anchored boats, stand against the depth of sea and sky; her song accentuates the depths and the distance of these inhuman and "ever-hooded" phenomena.

The imagination is this song and these points of light, "Fixing emblazoned zones and fiery poles, / Arranging, deepening, enchanting night" but it also encompasses the blue depths of sky and sea. The stars of the night sky are arranged by the human lights

---

[9] "World" here suggests the meaning of Heidegger's thought that the artwork erects (*aufstellen*) a world, and light is revealed in space by the creation of this world. Simultaneously, earth is brought forward into the light of this revealed world. The artwork "causes neither world nor earth but captures them in its repose. This repose, however, is the peak of dynamism: it is the strife between the world and the earth." (Vycinnas 129)

that chart them. The imagination picks out these points of light – its acts are all fundamentally this single act of replicating itself: the blue of the imagination is made visible by the figures of light set against it. It is a shifting processional of points of light which Polyphemus begins to discern in his mirage of Galatea, as he hovers on the boundary of his monstrosity, gazing, like Caliban, into a more spacious world. The sea, like the night sky, is the necessary field of imaginative activity, a fathomless reality that almost becomes "world" with the creative act, as in Stevens' "The Man with the Blue Guitar": "First one beam, then another, then / A thousand are radiant in the sky." (172) The singing girl is the "single artificer of the world" and yet there is the suggestion of reciprocity. The song occurs just there, in consciousness of that sounding depth of sub-meaning, of source and origin. The song is native to that shore-world, as Prospero is native to his sea-wreathed island.

The Cyclops too is a singer and an artificer, who places himself upon a promontory, looking towards the sea, thereby suggesting the primacy of the human mind over the reality it contemplates. He is an arbiter posed on a boundary. His song is incomplete. It fails to conjure a world, and it fails to overcome the abysmal self. The girl's song occurs at the boundary between sea and earth, but it has entered into a complicity with the impenetrable reality before it. The sea does not harden into a mirror, but persists in its own "meaningless plungings," just as the sky persists in its airiness, its sweep and blue recession. The song of the girl makes a world because it is not a "blind promontory" raised over and against the basic inarticulacy of the sea, for the striving self has been effaced in the act of the song. We hear the sea through the "word by word" song of the girl, and we see the night's deep design through the heraldry of lights. But the sea and the sky remain themselves despite the "rage for order" which devises "ghostlier demarcations, keener sounds." The ego has retreated in the act of the song – it bends to the primacy of artifice and the "self" of the sea, the sea which is now a world.

That Cyclopean song by itself does not become a world in Stevens' sense, does not achieve the detachment necessary to become a heraldry of sea and song, dark sky and lights, is the heart of the Cyclopean matter, its tenacious blindness. It should by now be clear that by posing the "reino de la espuma" against the "caverna profunda" Góngora offers a critique of the subjective self as a privileged center of meaning. The baroque poet's ostentatious "movimiento hacia afuera," his preoccupation with sensuous experience, is not merely a move in the direction of the ornate, the decorative, the "supplemental," but a dispossession of the ego in favor of another mode of consciousness, the mode of the world beyond the ego, hospitable to the attentive, meditative mind.

The concern with relation in Góngora's poem frequently presents itself in spatial configurations which involve a figure set against the larger field of the "reino de la espuma." By these arrangements the poet makes a miniaturized statement about artistic composition. A light element – spume, eyes, stars, white feet, pearls, quicksilver – is placed as the pictorial "figure," advancing from a secondary "background" element – earth, the "cloak" of plumage, sky, shells, tree trunks, etc. – which receives definition from the first. The following passages offer examples of this crucial pattern of relation:

1. In the first stanza, the silvering of the Sicilian peninsula by the frothy Sicilian sea locats the action of the poem: "Donde espumoso el mar sicilïano / el pie argenta de plata al Lilibeo."[10] This is the first appearance of *aphros* as an aesthetic agent which *adorns*, and so makes the cliff of the peninsula a part of its cosmos, cosmos as aesthetic arrangement. Note that sea-spume itself is a figure against a deep ground, and the placement of the adjective "espumoso" before its noun gives it the weight and prominence of a noun-subject, as though it were acting independently as the agent of "argenta."
2. In Stanza 13 the image of the hundred-eyed peacock appears as a metaphor for the nymph's luminosity and splendor, and is allowed to unfold in Stanzas 46-47 so that we are aware of the golden eyes against the blue plumage, compared to stars against a sapphire sky.

---

[10] Góngora's contemporaries enjoyed citing the apparent redundancy in "argenta de plata," as though the poet were illogically describing a literal alloy rather than a metaphorical boundary between sea and earth. Alonso, defending the poet, points out that *argentar* had come to mean simply "to apply a metallic shine." But the poet may simply have wished to intensify the silver which surges against the peninsula, as the active silver of poetic consciousness as it moves against the literal, solid and opaque matter of the cliff.

CONCLUSION 123

3. In Stanza 47 the white feet of Galatea transform the shells to silver, and cause them to generate pearls. The shells are a foreground against a background of sand which the nymph magically treads.
4. The quicksilver blood and bones of Acis whiten tree trunks, flowers and sand – the heavier, inactive components of the scenario of metamorphosis.

Two kinds of light figuration operate in these passages: the first, a more static presentation, similar to heraldry, places a figure – the light of the eye/star – against a field of blueness – plumage or sky. In the second type a luminous agent: sea-spume, white feet, quicksilver – transforms the appearance of another, more opaque substance: the base of the cliff, shells, tree roots, sand, flowers. In the Venusian image of the white foot, the metamorphosis is twofold: at the touch of Galatea's foot the shells in the sand turn to silver, and in turn breed pearls. In the cluster spume-white feet-quicksilver the notion of generation or regeneration is present, linked to the generative power of the sea; in the conceits involving the figured plumage and sky, generation has crystallized into design.

We find a similar unfolding of figure and ground placed in the first *silva* of the *Soledades:*

> Era del año la estación florida
> en que el mentido robador de Europa
> – media luna las armas de su frente,
> y el Sol todos los rayos de su pelo –
> luciente honor del cielo
> en campos de zafiro pace estrellas.
>
> [It was the flowery season of the year
> in which Europa's perjured robber strays
> – whose brow the arms of the half-moon adorn,
> the sun the shining armor of his hide –
> through sapphire fields to feast on stellar corn.]

The sequence typically demands an active effort on the part of the reader to untangle not only the periphrasis but the layered images. The "field" of the "flowery season" of the year in these lines is the "campos de zafiro," composed of two superimposed elements: the "sapphire fields" of the sky and the pastures of earth. The bull who marks the advent of spring and who is himself marked by both solar and lunar light, grazes on stars, which are also the flowers of the *campos*, fields. The passage, like those cited in the *Polifemo*, not only includes a figure-ground arrangement, but also links buoyancy and light to the weight and force of the telluric bull. And the space-confounding image of the grazing bull is characteristic of a poet who refuses to confine himself to one world, and who is at home at the boundary or margin of worlds, "el margen donde para / del espumoso mar su pie ligera."[11]

In both the *Polifemo* and the *Soledades* a locale is announced which takes its light from an efflorescence of the organic, and is in turn a model for poesis. *Physis* is *logos*, the ultimate source of thought and meaning. As Stevens himself remarked, "all our ideas come from the natural world." (*Opus Posthumous* 103) The blue or blue-green field of sky and ocean is the spatial correlative of the *basso profundo* of Cyclopean song; each is a "ground," – the one spatial, the other temporal – and an enigma of depth.[12] The blue of sea and sky is already the blue of the space of the imagination; sea-spume and stars appear as figures against this blue expanse, like the "Angels of rain and lightning" which Shelley sees spread against the blue surface of the sea in "Ode to the West Wind (II. 18-19)

Turning again to Stevens we find another point at which he helps to explicate the Gongorine text, and the "flowering season" of Góngora's baroque poetics.[13] It is the very poise of spring

---

[11] The *Soledad segunda* opens upon the shifting boundary between an estuary and the sea.

[12] Spengler compares the use of the colors blue and green in western painting to the *basso continuo* in the baroque orchestra: the blue-green tones support the ensemble of colors as the deep sonority of the *basso continuo* (played on a clavier, organ or lute reinforced by a bass gamba, violoncello or bassoon) supported the efflorescence of the treble melody. Blue, in western painting, is "perspective color," and "always stands in relation to the dark, the unillumined, the unactual. It does not press in on us, it pulls us out into the remote. An 'enchanting nothingness' Goethe calls it in his *Farbenlehre*." (246)

[13] The "flowering season" is Gongorine language as it attends to "el luzir en las cosas," the light in things. In *On the Way to Language* Heidegger's Japanese interlocutor elucidates the meaning of the Japanese *Koto ba*, in such a way that it suggests language as a flowering. *Koto ba* includes meanings equivalent to graciousness (compared to the Greek *Charis*, bringing forth, and flowering (leaves

which Stevens evokes in "The Motive for Metaphor," the delicate balance of hiddenness and disclosure which captivates the poet's mind: "... the half colors of quarter-things / the slightly brighter sky, the melting clouds, / the single bird, the obscure moon –" (288) Spring is the season of becoming, of the not yet achieved form, not yet subject to the "weight of primary noon" and its unrelenting light.[14] Neither is it subject to decay, but like the Dawn goddess in the *Rig Veda* it is always coming forward, always an advent of light. The flowering season is a fiction hovering between the invisibility of its own dark roots and the advancing light of Helios with its relentless exposures. Like the fugitive nymph who recoils from an overbearing suitor, the poet and the poem are in retreat from the glare and weaponry of a shadowless reality

> shrinking from
> the weight of primary noon,
> the ABC of being,
> the ruddy temper, the hammer
> of red and blue, the hard sound –
> steel against intimation – the sharp flash,
> the vital, arrogant, fatal, dominant X.
>
> (288)

Of the two poets it is Góngora who unexpectedly seems closest to a romantic conception of mind and nature correspondence; but his organicism does not so much anticipate Coleridge or Schelling as it recalls the "fluid physics" of Lucretius' *De rerum natura*. Góngora's nymph, evocative of fluid, circulating light, reminds us of the poet's activity of mediation between sky and earth, earth and sea, levity and gravity, disclosure and hiddenness. The poet's self-effacement is a necessary adjunct to this act of mediation in which he pays tribute to the multiple lights of the world, the "light in things" which is independent of and prior to the light of his own discernment of them. *Aphros* provides the aesthetic light of the

---

and petals). (43-44) Poetry, in Heidegger's view, is the medium through which language is revealed as *Koto ba*.

[14] Conversely, the journeying Crispin of Stevens' "The Comedian as the Letter C" spurns the spring season and its efflorescence as "A time abhorrent to the nihilist / Or searcher for the fecund minimum, / The moonlight fiction disappeared." (*CP* 35-36)

poem, which appears as spume and stars, swans and eyes and quicksilver, as points of light which rise like Aphrodite from the blue depths of the imagination.

The line of the plot leads to metamorphosis, but the sea which receives Acis as river suggests a circular movement to the poem: we are returned to the "mar siciliano" and its recurrent surge against the peninsula. The sequence of metaphors which are variants of this primary action of sea-spume culminates in this reception of the transformed Acis by the sea. The denouement of Góngora's fable is faithful to his art of excess, drawing its dominant hyperboles into decisive confrontation. For metamorphosis is the monster of poetry, the violence of art which opposes the violence of reality. It is the culminating act of poetic imagination in response to the culminating act of violence, whose rhetorical sign here is hyperbaton:

> Con violencia desgajó, infinita
> la mayor punta de la excelsa roca
> que el joven, sobre quien la precipita,
> urna es mucha, pirámide no poca.
> (489-492)

[The Cyclops, to prodigious effort stirred,
From the high cliff a massive fragment rent
Which, hurled below on Acis, soon conferred
An ample urn, and no light monument.]

The adjective *infinita,* torn from its noun by the interloping finite verb, gains emphasis from its placement at the end of the line after a pause, and spreads its boundlessness onto the massive rock of the second line, which the giant breaks off from the towering cliff. The adjective is placed as a pivot between the nouns *violencia* and *punta,* the sharp point of the huge rock, seeming to modify both in a grammatical ambiguity favored by the poet. The impulse, the act, and the missile which is used to fulfill that act are all meant to seem "infinita." The poet then quickly contracts the image, and the prodigious rock coheres into alternating shapes which are artifacts: urn, pyramid. Violence thus seems to come to rest, achieving the closure of these sealed containers. But the extremity of its onset poses an "infinite" challenge to an entire world, not only of the shattered bower of pastoral, but to poetry itself and the suspension it can create – Stevens' metaphorical ivory floor in the air with its peacock and darting lights. The weight of the stone is infinite, and total. It destroys both by its propulsion, its weight and finally by its circumscription, as its substance not only crushes but surrounds its object like a tomb. It is the "weight of primary noon" – a heavy light, the searching, pitiless eye falling upon its victim.

This shattering act of infinite violence is the sudden intervention of the massively "literal" into the poem's field of metaphorical reality. As such it requires an act of equal force to defeat it and so re-compose the world. Violence is surely always a cliché, a radical assault on meaning by means of vehement, premature closure.[15] Polyphemus is not, therefore, the iconoclast of the pastoral tradition, which might be seen to offer itself, like Charles Stuart, as an iconic victim of deconstructive energy, but rather himself becomes a cliché shattered by the force of poetry. While Góngora's pastoral vision is precarious and even unbalanced by the hyperbolic presence of the Cyclops (Cascardi 130), the jealous violence of the giant is only superficially a symbolic destruction of that vision.[16] It is in fact a rigidification, one of the supreme clichés of human culture, the "mayor punta" of a suffocating stone pyramid. It is this "infinite violence," marking, a it does, the failure of the imagination (in the disrupted song), and not the failure of the flexible pastoral mode, which suffers oblivion in the poem. It meets the fate of all clichés exploded by the pressure of artistic vision.

The self-conscious Gongorine text moves poetry to the extreme edge of language, to the point where it approaches the closure and calm of painting, sculpture or architecture. This effect is partly achieved through a concentration on words themselves as objects of beauty, as things and qualities: *espuma, lucientes, purpúreas, pavón, carro de cristal, campos de plata, salamandria del sol;* as Jorge Guillén remarked, language itself is the goal of the poem: "All his

---

[15] Stevens: "Reality is a cliché from which we escape by metaphor. It is only au pays de la metaphore qu'on est poete." (*Opus Posthumous* 179)

[16] Cascardi has seen Góngora's Cyclops as the "primary instrument of the narrating poet's destruction of the ideal pastoral world." (133) He notes that the Cyclops' song is structurally similar to the poem's introductory stanzas, "hence, Polifemo imitates Góngora himself" and the two voices are seen to converge at the end of the poem, when the poet resumes his tale: "As Góngora has Polifemo brutally kill Acis, the destruction of the pastoral world that was begun in the grandiose delusions of the Cyclops' song is brought to completion."

energy is concentrated on exploiting the inexhaustible mine of words." (31) The concentration of expressive power in each word renders his poetic world both translucent and condensed, suggesting the brilliance, density and self-enclosure of a gem. Gongorine language, therefore, seems to come close to eluding the fundamental tension of language as a never-completed trajectory between subject and object, seeming to sever itself from its origins, entering into the "circle of solitude" which Rilke names as the sphere of the work of art.

We can grasp the nature of this act of self-overcoming more easily when we compare Góngora's verse to a well-known sonnet by John Donne which begins:

> Batter my heart, three person'd God; for you
> As yet but knocke, breathe, shine, and seek to mend;
> That I may rise, and stand, o'erthrow mee, and bend
> Your force, to breake, blowe, burn and make me new.
> *Holy Sonnets: Divine Meditations* I, 14.

For Gracián, we recall, verbs are the "nerve" of good style, and Donne offers here a particularly dynamic illustration of Gracián's precept; for he repeatedly exploits the "intense profundity" of the verb, which, according to the Jesuit theorist, "engulfs" the reader in an attempt to pull him down into meaning. Here it is the "three person's God" who is the quarry stalked by a succession of strenuous verbs. But the intended object of the verbs is the poet himself, who is also their subject, the originating consciousness of their vehemence; they stage an anguished appeal for shock therapy by a Divine Person whose rough assaults are meant to restore to authenticity and wholeness a soul fallen to "your enemie."

But what occurs in Donne's invitation to violent spiritual reconstruction is a linguistic battering against the ineffable. The ineffable does not, cannot, appear in any guise at all. Its advent is infinitely postponed, an enigmatic horizon that serves only to lure forth an artifice sprung from yearning. The plea to "enthrall," and to "ravish" (13-14) the speaker, and the unfulfilled expectation carried by the last lines, "Except you 'enthrall mee, never shall be free, / Nor ever chast, except you ravish mee" represents language at its furthest point from what Rilke meant by the closure of the plastic arts. It vaults out of privation, never achieving its goal of release into the saving impersonality here figured as the "three person'd God." This is a striking illustration of language as the net that is always in the act of being cast, never coming to rest upon its object, the object of its willing. And in fact the poet is here involved in representing the central dilemma of language, which he casts into the framework of metaphysical anguish for closure.

The degree of formal, gem-like perfection achieved by Góngora is linked to his strategy of enclosing the passionate, willing self in the negative mask of the Cyclops. The personification of his own desire in this figure symbolically frees his language to achieve its aesthetic end, moving in the direction of the silence of the plastic arts.[17] And yet his genius lies partly in his ability to encompass the motives and effects of both the plastic and the temporal arts, posing the fulfilled mood of the former against the restless movement of the latter. And the point of intersection of the two moods is the image of Acis, the "body" of pastoral, transformed to a river – an image of flux and resolution.

We have been considering the figurative places of *aesthesis* in a baroque poem. The aesthetic place, the place which supports and reflects and provides models for the creative mind, is imagined to be at the boundary of earth and sea, the generative place. In a secondary sense, the "place" of *aisthesis* is an imagined space akin to the pastoral *locus amoenus*. What is the composition of this locus? It is clear from both his major poems that Góngora was drawn to certain configurations of space: a field (*campo*) or background which is sky and / or sea, sapphire and silver fields which generate their own foregrounds: *aphros, espuma*, in turn a generative substance embodied in the goddess / nymph, the animating principle of an entire landscape, the "reino de la espuma," extended to a pastoral locale. This is the "field" of poetry – the place where nature – meadows, cliffs, rocks, trees, fish, apples, acorns, and a river – become ec-static. That is, they stand outside themselves,

---

[17] The comment Helen Vendler makes of Roland Barthe's aestheticism is pertinent here: "... his devotion to the aesthetic was not only a natural inclination but also a fully ethical commitment. The aesthetic, by having an inherent plurality of language, tone, and viewpoint, defends the mind against its own premature anxiety for closure. A mind like that of Barthes, attuned to the aesthetic, accepts its own transiency in the processional of historical belief and rejoices in its own capacity for incorporating, over its lifetime, more than a single truth." (50)

consummate, exact, transformed. The enveloping "outside" is the space which Góngora devises, the space of the poem which allows for the maximum disclosure of these things. Things become fully apparent in their *superfluity* of form, pointing the way beyond life as mere necessity or function. They are ecstatic in their removal from inner necessity, in their emptying out. The ancient Sicilian hills are transformed by the "granos de oro," the golden harvest of grain bestowed by Ceres; the myrtle trees at the stream's edge are transformed by the current's white foam into two herons. (211)

These ecstatic forms nonetheless do not inhabit a Yeatsian Byzantium, and it is important to note the difference between these two formulations of ideal, symbolic places. For Yeats' ideal city of the imagination differs from Góngora's visionary islands in its renunciation of organic form:

> Once out of nature I shall never take
> My bodily form from any natural thing,
> But such a form as Grecian goldsmiths make
> Of hammered gold and gold enamelling
> To keep a drowsy Emperor awake;
> Or set upon a golden bough to sing
> To lords and ladies of Byzantium
> Of what is past, or passing or to come.
>   "Sailing to Byzantium,"
>   *Collected Poems* 192

Yeats imagines a transformation by fire, a metallurgy of the soul by which he will be gathered into the "artifice of eternity." The urgency of his plea "consume my heart away" recalls Donne's negotiations with his God, in which he too pleads to be remade, except that Yeats, more happily, contrives a glamorous home for the soul, abstract, yet glittering, enamelled, as *glacé* as Baudelaire's ideal cosmic adjective. The tortured introspection of the Protestant Donne never resolves itself into an image, or thing. He never discovers, in Michel Serre's sense, the beatitude of the object which provides the escape from the binding and sometimes violent network of relations. (*Hermes* 123)

The stylization of Yeats' empire of immutable forms seems akin to Góngora's lapidary world of hard lights, and in fact one of Góngora's detractors, Lope de Vega, refers disdainfully to the conspicuously polished texture of his verse as "poesía de ataujía." (Collard 90) "Ataujía," a Moorish term, denoted metalwork in which objects of silver, gold, or some other metal were coated with a surface of colored enamel. And yet the silver and sapphire fields of *Gongorismo* do not reflect a "glory of changeless metal" but a fluid field of creation and metamorphosis, serving a the ground for a poetry of becoming. The transformation of Acis into a river does not so much purge the soul of its "mire and blood" ("Byzantium") as it gives it an earthly home under a lunar light, the light of the poet which Yeats elsewhere celebrates.

We need, then, to change our own manner of looking at Góngora's pronounced formalism. In this effort we can count on a number of astute guides, many of whom, cited throughout this study, have never read Góngora. One such tutor, and one who has read Góngora with exceptional insight, is D. S. Carne-Ross, whose essay on the poet is indispensable for the task of re-reading the poet who alone created, within Catholic baroque Spain, a convincing alternative to the monumental and corrosive metaphysics and ideology of that very world. Carne-Ross suggests that Góngora has written "some of the necessary stanzas" of that "great poem of the earth" whose advent Stevens hoped to witness. For that remarkable task he purged his voice of the all-too-human insistencies of Cyclopean song, and turned his keen gaze to the "light in things."

WORKS CITED

Alonso, Dámaso. *Góngora y 'El Polifemo'*. 3 vols. Madrid: Gredos, 1960.
Arendt, Hannah. *The Life of the Mind*. Ed. Mary McCarthy. New York: Harcourt, Brace, Jovanovich, 1977.
Baudelaire, Charles. *Œuvres completes*. Ed. Y. G. Le Dantec and Claude Pichois. Paris: Gallimard, 1961.
Benjamin, Walter. *The Origin of German Tragic Drama*. Trans. John Osborne. London: NLB, 1977.
Beverley, John R. *Aspects of Góngora's 'Soledades'*. Purdue University Monographs in Romance Languages. Amsterdam: John Benjamins B.V.: 1980.
Bleznick, Donald. *Quevedo*. New York: Twayne, 1972.
Brown, Norman O. ed. and trans. *Hesiod's Theogony*. New York: Bobbs-Merril, 1953.
Burke, Kenneth. *A Grammar of Motives*. Berkeley: U of California P, 1969.
Calderón de la Barca. *Autos sacramentales*. Vol. 1. Ed. A. Valbuena Prat. Clásicos Castellanos, 4th ed. Madrid: 1958. 2 vols.
Carne-Ross, D. S. "Dark with Excessive Bright: Four Ways of Looking at Góngora." *Instaurations. Essays in and out of Literature: Pindar to Pound*. Berkeley: U of California P, 1979.
Cascardi, Anthony. "The Exit from Arcadia. Revaluation of the Pastoral in Virgil, Garcilaso and Góngora." *JHP* Winter 1980: 119-141.
Céard, Jean. *La nature et les prodiges: l'insolite au XVIe siecle en France*. Geneve: Librairie Droz, 1977.
Cervantes, Miguel de. *Don Quixote*. Trans. John Ormsby. Eds. Joseph R. Jones and Kenneth Douglas. New York: W. W. Norton, 1981.
Ciocchini, Hector. *Góngora y la tradición de los emblemas*. Bahía Blanca: Universidad nacional del sur, 1960.
Clark, Kenneth. *Landscape into Art*. London: John Murray, 1952.
Collard, Andrée. *'Nueva poesía': conceptismo, culteranismo en la crítica española*. Madrid: Castalia, 1967.
———. "La 'herejía' de Góngora." *Hispanic Review* 36 (1968): 328-337.
Deleuze, Gille. *Logique du sens*. Paris: Editions de Minuit, 1969.
Donne, John. *Poetry and Prose*. Ed. Frank J. Warnke. New York: Random House, 1967.
Euripides. *Cyclops*. Trans. W. Arrowsmith. *Euripides*. Ed. R. Lattimore. Chicago: U of Chicago P, 1955-59.
Ferguson, George. *Signs and Symbols in Christian Art*. New York: Oxford UP, 1961.

Ficino, Marsilio. *The Book of Life (De Vita Triplici)*. Trans. Charles Boer. U of Dallas, Irving, Texas: Spring, 1980.
———. *Letters*. Trans. Language Dept. School of Economic Science, London. Vol. 2. South Carolina: Attic Press, 1978.
Foucault, Michel. *Discipline and Punish: The Birth of the Prison*. Trans. Alan Sheridan. New York: Pantheon, 1977.
Friederich, Paul. *The Meaning of Aphrodite*. Chicago and London: U of Chicago P, 1978.
Friedlander, Max. *Landscape, Portrait, Still Life: Their Origin and Development*. Trans. R. F. C. Hull. New York: Phil. Library n.d.
Freud, Sigmund. *New Introductory Lectures on Psycho-analysis*. Trans. W. J. H. Sprott. Ed. Ernest Jones. London: Hogarth, 1957.
Giegerich, Wolfgang. "Hospitality towards the Gods in an Ungodly Age: Philemon-Faust-Jung." *Spring*, 1984: 61-75.
Góngora, Luis de. *Obras completas*. Ed. Millé. Madrid: Aguilar, 1972.
———. *The Solitudes*. Trans. Edward Meryon Wilson. New York: Las Americas, 1965.
Gracián, Baltasar. *Agudeza y arte de ingenio*. Madrid: Castalia, 1969. 2 vols.
———. *El criticón*. Madrid: Espasa-Calpe, 1971. 3 vols.
———. *El discreto*. Buenos Aires: Academia Argentina de letras, 1960.
Guillén, Jorge. *Language and Poetry. Some Poets of Spain*. Cambridge: Harvard UP, 1961.
Hesiod, *Theogony*. Ed. and Trans. M. L. West. Oxford: Clarendon, 1966.
H. D. *Trilogy*. New York: New Directions, 1973.
Heidegger, Martin. "The Age of the World View." *The Question Concerning Technology and Other Essays*. Trans. William Lovitt. New York: Harper and Row, 1977.
———. *Being and Time*. Trans. John Macquarrie and Edward Robinson. New York: Harper and Row, 1962.
——— and Eugen Fink. *Heraclitus Seminar*. 1966-67. Trans. Charles H. Siebert. U of Alabama P, 1979.
———. *On the Way to Language*. Trans. Albert Hofstadter. New York: Harper and Row, 1971.
———. *Poetry Language Thought*. Trans. Albert Hofstadlter. New York: Harper and Row, 1971.
Henn, Thomas Rice. *Last Essays*. Gerard's Cross, Buckinghamshire: Colin Smythe, 1976.
Hillman, James. "Anima Mundi: The Return of the Soul to the World." *Spring* (1982): 71-93.
———. *The Dream and the Underworld*. New York: Harper and Row, 1979.
———. "Silver and the White Earth" I, *Spring* (1980): 21-47.
Homer, *The Odyssey*. Trans. Richmond Lattimore. New York: Harper and Row, 1975.
———. *The Iliad*. Trans. Richmond Lattimore. Chicago: U of Chicago P, 1961.
Jammes, Robert. *Etudes sur l'œuvre poétique de Don Luis de Góngora*. Bordeaux: Fénix et fils, 1967.
Kant, Immanuel. *Critique of Pure Reason*. Trans. J. M. D. Meiklejohn. New York: Collier, 1902.
Kermode, Frank. *Wallace Stevens*. Edinburgh and London: Oliver and Boyd, 1960.
Knight, W. F. *Vergil: Epic and Anthropology, Comprising Vergil's Troy, Cumaean Gates and the Holy City of the East*. Ed. John D. Christie. New York: Barnes and Noble, 1967.

Klibansky, Raymond, Erwin Panofsky and Fritz Saxl. *Saturn and Melancholy: Studies in the History of Natural Philosophy, Religion and Art.* London: Thomas Nelson, 1964.
Krell, David Farrell. "Art and Truth in Raging Discord: Heidegger and Nietzsche on the Will to Power." *Martin Heidegger and the Question of Literature: towards a Post-Modern Literary Hermeneutics.* Ed. William V. Spanos. Bloomington: Indiana UP, 1979. 38-52.
Lovejoy, Arthur. *The Great Chain of Being.* Cambridge: Harvard UP, 1976.
Lucretius. *On the Nature of the Universe (De rerum natura).* Trans. and Intro. R. E. Latham. New York: Penguin-Viking, 1981.
Machado, Antonio. *Obras completas.* Buenos Aires: Losada, 1973.
Mann, Thomas. *Dr. Faustus.* Trans. H. T. Lowe-Porter. New York: Random House, 1971.
Maravall, José Antonio. *Culture of the Baroque: Analysis of a Historical Structure.* Trans. Terry Cochran. Minneapolis: U of Minnesota P, 1986.
Martínez Arancon, Ana. *La batalla en torno a Góngora. Selección de textos.* Barcelona: A. Bosch: 1978.
Marvell, Andrew. *The Complete English Poems.* Ed. Elizabeth Story Donno. New York: S. Martin's P, 1972.
Milton, John. *Paradise Lost. Complete Poems and Major Prose.* Ed. Merrit Y. Hughes. Indianapolis: Odyssey P, 1978.
Nietzsche, Friederich. *The Birth of Tragedy.* Trans. and Ed. Walter Kaufmann. New York: Vintage-Random House, 1967.
———. *The Gay Science.* Trans. and Ed. Walter Kaufmann. New York: Vintage-Random House, 1974.
———. *Thus Spoke Zarathustra.* Trans. and Ed. Walter Kaufmann. New York: Penguin-Viking, 1966.
Nøjgaard, Morten. *Elévation et expansion. Les deux dimensions de Baudelaire.* Odense: UP, 1973.
Orgel, Stephen. *The Illusion of Power. Political Theater in the English Renaissance.* Berkeley: U of California P, 1975.
Ovid. *Metamorphoses.* Trans. Rolfe Humphries. Bloomington: Indiana UP, 1955.
Pabst, Walter. *La creación gongorina en los poemas 'Polifemo' y 'Soledades'.* Revista de filología 80. Madrid, 1966.
Parker, A. A. *'Polyphemus and Galaetea': A Study in the Interpretation of a Baroque Poem.* Edinburgh: UP, 1977.
Portmann, Adolf. "What Living Form Means to Us." *Spring* (1982): 27-38.
Plato, *Laws.* Trans. Trevor J. Saunders. New York: Penguin-Viking, 1970.
Rilke, Rainier Maria. *Selected Works.* Trans. G. Craig Houston. Vol. 1. London: Hogarth, 1954.
Anna Rist, trans. and ed. *The Poems of Theocritus.* Chapel Hill: U of North Carolina P, 1978.
Rosenmeyer, Thomas G. *The Green Cabinet. Theocritus and the European Pastoral Lyric.* Berkeley: U of California P, 1967.
Rousset, Jean. *La littérature de l'age baroque en France. Circé et le Paon.* Paris: Jose Corti, 1954.
Schopenhauer, Artur. *The World as Will and Representation.* Trans. E. F. J. Payne. Vol. 1. New York: Dover, 1969. 2 vols.
Scott, Charles. *Boundaries in Mind.* New York: Crossroad, 1982.
Scoular, Kitty. *Natural Magic. Studies in the Presentation of Nature in English Poetry.* New York: Oxford UP, 1965.
Segal, Hanna. "A Psychoanalytical Approach to Aesthetics." *Int. Journal of Psych.* 23 (1952): 196-207.

Serres, Michel. *Hermes: Literature, Science, Philosophy.* Ed. Josue V. Harari and David F. Bell. Baltimore: Johns Hopkins, 1983.
Smith, Paul Julian. "Barthes, Góngora and Non-sense." *PMLA* 101, no. 1 (Jan. 1986): 82-94.
Spengler, Oswald. *The Decline of the West.* Trans. Charles Francis Atkinson. Vol. 1. New York: Knopf, 1926. 2 vols.
Stevens, Wallace. "A Collect of Philosophy." Peter A. Brazeau. "A 'Collect of Philosophy': The Difficulty of Finding What Would Suffice." *Wallace Stevens: A Celebration.* Ed. Frank Doggett and Robert Buttel. New Jersey: Princeton UP, 1980.
———. *Collected Poems.* New York: Knopf, 1978.
———. *The Necessary Angel.* New York: Random House, 1951.
———. *Opus Posthumous.* Ed. Samuel French. London: Morse, 1959.
Suhr, Elmer G. *Venus de Milo the Spinner.* New York: Exposition Press, 1958.
Vendler, Helen. "The Medley is the Message." *New York Review of Books* XXXIII 8 (May 8 1986): 44-50.
———. *Yeats' 'Vision' and the Later Plays.* Cambridge: Harvard UP, 1963.
Vilanova, Antonio. *Las fuentes y los temas del 'Polifemo' de Góngora.* R. F. E., Anejo LXVI. Madrid: 1957. 2 vols.
Virgil. *Georgics.* Trans. Smith Palmer Bovie. Chicago: U of Chicago P, 1956.
———. *The Aeneid.* Trans. Frank O. Copley. Indianapolis: Bobbs-Merril, 1975.
Vycinas, Vincent. *Earth and Gods: An Introduction to the Philosophy of Martin Heidegger.* The Hague: Martinus Nijhoff, 1961.
Worringer, Wilhelm. *Abstraction and Empathy: A Contribution to the Psychology of Style.* Trans. Michael Bullock. London: Routledge and Kegan Paul, 1953.
Yeats, W. B. *Collected Poems.* New York: MacMillan, 1956.
Zimmerman, Michael E. *Eclipse of Self: The Development of Heidegger's Concept of Authenticity.* London: Ohio UP, 1981.

NORTH CAROLINA STUDIES IN THE ROMANCE LANGUAGES AND LITERATURES
I.S.B.N. Prefix 0-8078-

Recent Titles

RICHARD SANS PEUR, EDITED FROM "LE ROMANT DE RICHART" AND FROM GILLES CORROZET'S "RICHART SANS PAOUR", by Denis Joseph Conlon. 1977. (No. 192). *-9192-4.*

MARCEL PROUST'S GRASSET PROOFS. *Commentary and Variants,* by Douglas Alden. 1978. (No. 193). *-9193-2.*

MONTAIGNE AND FEMINISM, by Cecile Insdorf. 1977. (No. 194). *-9194-0.*

SANTIAGO F. PUGLIA, AN EARLY PHILADELPHIA PROPAGANDIST FOR SPANISH AMERICAN INDEPENDENCE, by Merle S. Simmons. 1977. (No. 195). *-9195-9.*

BAROQUE FICTION-MAKING. A STUDY OF GOMBERVILLE'S "POLEXANDRE", by Edward Baron Turk. 1978. (No. 196). *-9196-7.*

THE TRAGIC FALL: DON ÁLVARO DE LUNA AND OTHER FAVORITES IN SPANISH GOLDEN AGE DRAMA, by Raymond R. MacCurdy. 1978. (No. 197). *-9197-5.*

A BAHIAN HERITAGE. An Ethnolinguistic Study of African Influences on Bahian Portuguese, by William W. Megenney. 1978. (No. 198). *-9198-3.*

"LA QUERELLE DE LA ROSE": Letters and Documents, by Joseph L. Baird and John R. Kane. 1978. (No. 199). *-9199-1.*

TWO AGAINST TIME. *A Study of the Very Present Worlds of Paul Claudel and Charles Péguy,* by Joy Nachod Humes. 1978. (No. 200). *-9200-9.*

TECHNIQUES OF IRONY IN ANATOLE FRANCE. Essay on *Les Sept Femmes de la Barbe-Bleue,* by Diane Wolfe Levy. 1978. (No. 201). *-9201-7.*

THE PERIPHRASTIC FUTURES FORMED BY THE ROMANCE REFLEXES OF "VADO (AD)" PLUS INFINITIVE, by James Joseph Champion. 1978. (No. 202). *-9202-5.*

THE EVOLUTION OF THE LATIN /b/-/ṷ/ MERGER: A Quantitative and Comparative Analysis of the *B-V* Alternation in Latin Inscriptions, by Joseph Louis Barbarino. 1978. (No. 203). *-9203-3.*

METAPHORIC NARRATION: THE STRUCTURE AND FUNCTION OF METAPHORS IN "A LA RECHERCHE DU TEMPS PERDU", by Inge Karalus Crosman. 1978. (No. 204). *-9204-1.*

LE VAIN SIECLE GUERPIR. A Literary Approach to Sainthood through Old French Hagiography of the Twelfth Century, by Phyllis Johnson and Brigitte Cazelles. 1979. (No. 205). *-9205-X.*

THE POETRY OF CHANGE: A STUDY OF THE SURREALIST WORKS OF BENJAMIN PÉRET, by Julia Field Costich. 1979. (No. 206). *-9206-8.*

NARRATIVE PERSPECTIVE IN THE POST-CIVIL WAR NOVELS OF FRANCISCO AYALA "MUERTES DE PERRO" AND "EL FONDO DEL VASO", by Maryellen Bieder. 1979. (No. 207). *-9207-6.*

RABELAIS: HOMO LOGOS, by Alice Fiola Berry. 1979. (No. 208). *-9208-4.*

"DUEÑAS" AND "DONCELLAS": A STUDY OF THE "DOÑA RODRÍGUEZ" EPISODE IN "DON QUIJOTE", by Conchita Herdman Marianella. 1979. (No. 209). *-9209-2.*

PIERRE BOAISTUAU'S "HISTOIRES TRAGIQUES": A STUDY OF NARRATIVE FORM AND TRAGIC VISION, by Richard A. Carr. 1979. (No. 210). *-9210-6.*

REALITY AND EXPRESSION IN THE POETRY OF CARLOS PELLICER, by George Melnykovich. 1979. (No. 211). *-9211-4.*

MEDIEVAL MAN, HIS UNDERSTANDING OF HIMSELF, HIS SOCIETY, AND THE WORLD, by Urban T. Holmes, Jr. 1980. (No. 212). *-9212-2.*

MÉMOIRES SUR LA LIBRAIRIE ET SUR LA LIBERTÉ DE LA PRESSE, introduction and notes by Graham E. Rodmell. 1979. (No. 213). *-9213-0.*

THE FICTIONS OF THE SELF. THE EARLY WORKS OF MAURICE BARRES, by Gordon Shenton. 1979. (No. 214). *-9214-9.*

When ordering please cite the *ISBN Prefix* plus the last four digits for each title.

Send orders to: University of North Carolina Press
P.O. Box 2288
CB# 6215
Chapel Hill, NC 27515-2288
U.S.A.

NORTH CAROLINA STUDIES IN THE ROMANCE LANGUAGES AND LITERATURES

I.S.B.N. Prefix 0-8078-

Recent Titles

CECCO ANGIOLIERI. A STUDY, by Gifford P. Orwen. 1979. (No. 215). *-9215-7.*
THE INSTRUCTIONS OF SAINT LOUIS: A CRITICAL TEXT, by David O'Connell. 1979. (No. 216). *-9216-5.*
ARTFUL ELOQUENCE, JEAN LEMAIRE DE BELGES AND THE RHETORICAL TRADITION, by Michael F. O. Jenkins. 1980. (No. 217). *-9217-3.*
A CONCORDANCE TO MARIVAUX'S COMEDIES IN PROSE, edited by Donald C. Spinelli. 1979. (No. 218). 4 volumes, *-9218-1* (set); *-9219-X* (v. 1); *-9220-3* (v. 2); *-9221-1* (v. 3); *-9222-X* (v. 4).
ABYSMAL GAMES IN THE NOVELS OF SAMUEL BECKETT, by Angela B. Moorjani. 1982. (No. 219). *-9223-8.*
GERMAIN NOUVEAU DIT HUMILIS: ÉTUDE BIOGRAPHIQUE, par Alexandre L. Amprimoz. 1983. (No. 220). *-9224-6.*
THE "VIE DE SAINT ALEXIS" IN THE TWELFTH AND THIRTEENTH CENTURIES: AN EDITION AND COMMENTARY, by Alison Goddard Elliot. 1983. (No. 221). *-9225-4.*
THE BROKEN ANGEL: MYTH AND METHOD IN VALÉRY, by Ursula Franklin. 1984. (No. 222). *-9226-2.*
READING VOLTAIRE'S "CONTES": A SEMIOTICS OF PHILOSOPHICAL NARRATION, by Carol Sherman. 1985. (No. 223). *-9227-0.*
THE STATUS OF THE READING SUBJECT IN THE "LIBRO DE BUEN AMOR", by Marina Scordilis Brownlee. 1985. (No. 224). *-9228-9.*
MARTORELL'S "TIRANT LO BLANCH": A PROGRAM FOR MILITARY AND SOCIAL REFORM IN FIFTEENTH-CENTURY CHRISTENDOM, by Edward T. Aylward. 1985. (No. 225). *-9229-7.*
NOVEL LIVES: THE FICTIONAL AUTOBIOGRAPHIES OF GUILLERMO CABRERA INFANTE AND MARIO VARGAS LLOSA, by Rosemary Geisdorfer Feal. 1986. (No. 226). *-9230-0.*
SOCIAL REALISM IN THE ARGENTINE NARRATIVE, by David William Foster. 1986. (No. 227). *-9231-9.*
HALF-TOLD TALES: DILEMMAS OF MEANING IN THREE FRENCH NOVELS, by Philip Stewart. 1987. (No. 228). *-9232-7.*
POLITIQUES DE L'ECRITURE BATAILLE/DERRIDA: le sens du sacré dans la pensée française du surréalisme à nos jours, par Jean-Michel Heimonet. 1987. (No. 229). *-9233-5.*
GOD, THE QUEST, THE HERO: THEMATIC STRUCTURES IN BECKETT'S FICTION, by Laura Barge. 1988. (No. 230). *-9235-1.*
THE NAME GAME. WRITING/FADING WRITER IN "DE DONDE SON LOS CANTANTES", by Oscar Montero. 1988. (No. 231). *-9236-X.*
GIL VICENTE AND THE DEVELOPMENT OF THE COMEDIA, by René Pedro Garay. 1988. (No. 232). *-9234-3.*
HACIA UNA POÉTICA DEL RELATO DIDÁCTICO: OCHO ESTUDIOS SOBRE "EL CONDE LUCANOR", por Aníbal A. Biglieri. 1989. (No. 233). *-9237-8.*
A POETICS OF ART CRITICISM: THE CASE OF BAUDELAIRE, by Timothy Raser. 1989. (No. 234). *-9238-6.*
UMA CONCORDÀNCIA DO ROMANCE "GRANDE SERTÃO: VEREDAS" DE JOÃO GUIMARÃES ROSA, by Myriam Ramsey and Paul Dixon. 1989. (No. 235). Microfiche, *-9239-4.*
CYCLOPEAN SONG: MELANCHOLY AND AESTHETICISM IN GÓNGORA'S "FÁBULA DE POLIFEMO Y GALATEA", by Kathleen Hunt Dolan. 1990. (No. 236). *-9240-8.*

When ordering please cite the *ISBN Prefix* plus the last four digits for each title.

Send orders to: University of North Carolina Press
P.O. Box 2288
CB# 6215
Chapel Hill, NC 27515-2288
U.S.A.

The Department of Romance Studies Digital Arts and Collaboration Lab at the University of North Carolina at Chapel Hill is proud to support the digitization of the North Carolina Studies in the Romance Languages and Literatures series.

www.ingramcontent.com/pod-product-compliance
Lightning Source LLC
Chambersburg PA
CBHW020419230426
43663CB00007BA/1232